The Mexican and Mexican American Experience in the 19th Century

+F1231.5 .M545 1989

Bilingual Press/Editorial Bilingüe

General Editor
 Gary D. Keller

Managing Editor
 Karen S. Van Hooft

Senior Editor
 Mary M. Keller

Assistant Editor
 Linda St. George Thurston

Editorial Board
 Juan Goytisolo
 Francisco Jiménez
 Eduardo Rivera
 Severo Sarduy
 Mario Vargas Llosa

Editorial Consultant
 Juliette L. Spence

Address:
Bilingual Review/Press
Hispanic Research Center
Arizona State University
Tempe, Arizona 85287

(602) 965-3867

The Mexican and Mexican American Experience in the 19th Century

Edited by
Jaime E. Rodríguez O.

Bilingual Press/Editorial Bilingüe
TEMPE, ARIZONA

© 1989 by Bilingual Press/Editorial Bilingüe
All rights reserved. No part of this publication may be reproduced in any manner without permission in writing, except in the case of brief quotations embodied in critical articles and reviews.

ISBN: 0-916950-93-X
Printed simultaneously in a softcover edition. ISBN: 0-916950-94-8

Library of Congress Catalog Card Number: 88-64099

PRINTED IN THE UNITED STATES OF AMERICA

Cover illustration by Denise Lehman

Acknowledgments

"Patriarchy and the Status of Women in the Late Nineteenth-Century Southwest" by Richard Griswold del Castillo is adapted from *La Familia: Chicano Families in the Urban Southwest 1848 to the Present* by Richard Griswold del Castillo. ©1984 by University of Notre Dame Press. Reprinted by permission.

Table of Contents

Introduction, *Jaime E. Rodríguez O.* ... 3

1 Down from Colonialism: Mexico's Nineteenth-Century Crisis, *Jaime E. Rodríguez O.* ... 7

2 Where Did All the Royalists Go? New Light on the Military Collapse of New Spain, 1810-1822, *Criston I. Archer* ... 24

3 Los liberales y la Iglesia, *Patricia Galeana de Valadés* ... 44

4 El pensamiento de los conservadores mexicanos, *María del Refugio González* ... 55

5 "Neither a borrower nor a lender be": Financial Constraints and the Treaty of Guadalupe Hidalgo, *Barbara A. Tenenbaum* ... 68

6 Patriarchy and the Status of Women in the Late Nineteenth-Century Southwest, *Richard Griswold del Castillo* ... 85

About the Contributors ... 101

Notes ... 103

Bibliography ... 119

Index ... 127

A
María Herrera-Sobek, Alejandro Morales y Eloy Rodríguez
Compañeros de muchas empresas universitarias

Acknowledgments

The publication of these essays owes much to the support and encouragement of a number of persons and institutions. The volume, like the symposium from which it originated, has been sponsored by the Mexico/Chicano Program of the University of California, Irvine. The Focused Research Program on Mexico/Chicano Area Studies and the University of California Consortium on Mexico and the United States provided financial support for both the symposium and this publication. I am grateful to the participants of the Symposium on the Mexican and the Mexican-American Experience in the Nineteenth Century—Silvia Arrom, Alberto Camarillo, Ricardo Romo, Paul Vanderwood, Linda Alexander Rodríguez, David Weber, Mario Rodríguez, Ramón Gutiérrez, Christon I. Archer, Patricia Galeana de Valadés, María del Refugio González, Barbara Tenenbaum, and Richard Griswold del Castillo—both for their participation in the symposium and their comments on the papers. I also thank my colleagues in the Mexico/Chicano Program: María Herrera-Sobek, Eloy Rodríguez, Alejandro Morales, and Luis Suárez Villa, who contributed to its success. In preparing this volume for publication, I have had the benefit of comments and assistance from Linda Alexander Rodríguez and William F. Sater. Geneva López-Irianni was a great help in coordinating the symposium and the papers for this volume. Finally, I am particularly grateful for the support and encouragement I received from Kendall Bailes, then Dean of the School of Humanities at UCI, and Patricia O'Brien, Chair of the Department of History.

Jaime E. Rodríguez O.

Introduction

Jaime E. Rodríguez O.

Although recent research has illuminated many areas of Mexican and Mexican-American history, the nineteenth century remains obscure. The period is important because it was during these decades that the Mexican republic was formed and the Mexican-American communities of the Southwest created.

A paradox confronts the historian of Mexico. The late eighteenth century, a brilliant period of prosperity and order, gave way to the poverty and chaos of the postindependence period. Alexander von Humboldt, who visited New Spain at the turn of the century, predicted that Mexico would become the colossus of North America. Early nineteenth-century Mexicans were also confident that their nation would become one of the great powers of the world. Yet, what began so auspiciously floundered in the period of postindependence chaos. Within a decade, Mexico was in turmoil, appearing unable to develop in the orderly manner of western Europe and the United States. The leading conservative, Lucas Alamán, attributed the nation's troubles to its having abandoned its Hispanic traditions, while the liberals, such as Lorenzo de Zavala, blamed the negative Spanish heritage for hindering the new nation's development. Until recently many historians accepted Zavala's assessment.

The contrast between the success of one former colony, the United States, and the failure of another, Mexico, has long confounded the efforts of historians to understand the creation and early development of the Mexican republic. Many have attributed the achievements of North Americans to their English heritage, Protestantism, and the frontier, while blaming the difficulties of Mexicans on their "feudal" Spanish heritage, their Catholicism, and their hacienda system. But as scholars probed more deeply, they have discovered that the evidence does not substantiate this simplistic thesis.

In May 1984, the Mexico/Chicano Program at the University of California, Irvine invited a group of scholars to examine "The Mexican and the Mexican-American Experience in the Nineteenth Century." Some of the papers presented at that symposium have been revised for publication. The essays in this volume examine many of the important problems which Mexico and Mexican-Americans faced in the nineteenth century: the contrast between colonial order and prosperity, and republican chaos and poverty; the protracted struggle for independence; the difficulties of national politics — liberalism versus conservatism; the role of the Church in the new Mexican nation; the country's financial crisis and the loss of more than half its national territory; and finally the changing role of women and the family as the century progressed.

The volume begins with my analysis of "Down From Colonialism: Mexico's Nineteenth-Century Crisis" which introduces some of the problems of the nineteenth century. It contrasts New Spain in 1800 with Mexico in the 1850s, inquiring why the once prosperous colony had fallen so low.

In his essay "Where Did All of the Royalists Go? New Light on the Military Collapse of New Spain, 1810–1822," Christon I. Archer discusses the fall of royal government from the perspective of the royalist army. In contrast to the vast literature on the insurgents, little has been written on the defenders of the colony. Professor Archer, who has written extensively on the colonial army, explains how "By the end of 1821, most royalists had become overnight patriots." This change of allegiance is extremely important because only the army had prevented New Spain from falling into the hands of the insurgents in 1810. The discontent and erosion of military discipline, which occurred during the decade-long guerrilla war of independence, had grave implications for the new Mexican nation.

Patricia Galeana de Valadés considers one of the most complex questions in nineteenth-century Mexican politics: the relations between "Los liberales y la Iglesia." The issue continues to vex scholars. In part, this is because many writers tend to equate liberalism with the ideology that triumphed in western Europe, particularly in England. This tendency fails to consider an indigenous or Hispanic liberalism that differs significantly from the "standard" liberalism of western Europe. Just as Catholic Europe experienced a "Catholic Enlightenment" which differed from the better known Enlightenment, Spain and Mexico evolved a "Catholic liberalism." While early Hispanic liberals, among them prominent Mexicans, embraced many of the tenets of Western European liberalism, they nonetheless retained their respect for the

Church and its role in society. Only later, as the century progressed, did a new generation of liberals conclude that the Church resisted progress. Consequently, the "new liberals" and the "new conservatives" clashed over the nature of the Church in Mexican society. Professor Galeana de Valadés provides an excellent synthesis of these questions.

In a related essay, María del Refugio González examines "El pensamiento de los conservadores mexicanos." Although the term *liberal* was coined in the Spanish Cortes of 1810, the concept of conservative did not develop in Mexico until after independence. Professor González demonstrates that conservatives formed their ideas long before they formed political groupings. She examines the thought of two generations of conservatives during the first half of the nineteenth century, concluding that "no es desacertado para analizar el pensamiento conservador partir de los principios de la religión católica y el modo en que estos principios se manifiestan en la constitución de la familia, la sociedad y el Estado."

Lack of resources hampered the early governments of postindependence Mexico. In her essay " 'Neither a borrower nor a lender be': Financial Constraints and the Treaty of Guadalupe Hidalgo," Barbara A. Tenenbaum examines the fiscal crises of early nineteenth-century Mexico in order to explain why Mexican leaders accepted the treaty of Guadalupe Hidalgo that stripped the nation of more than half its territory. Why, in other words, did Mexicans not continue to fight a guerrilla war against the invading yankees. The answer is surprising. *Agiotistas,* money lenders, many of them foreigners, pressured the Mexican moderates to accept the humiliating peace so that the government could use the United States' indemnity to pay its debt to them. Among the leading agiotistas, were citizens of Britain.

The final essay, Richard Griswold del Castillo's "Patriarchy and the Status of Women in the Late Nineteenth-Century Southwest," focuses on the role of women and the family. Professor Griswold del Castillo places the society of the Southwest within the context of both Mexican and United States history. He demonstrates how the people of the frontier gradually replaced the values of Mexican society with new American values. In each instance women struggled for a better life in societies that were both patriarchal and modernizing.

The authors of these essays and other scholars are expanding our understanding of nineteenth-century Mexico. A once-confused and little-studied period is now attracting more interest. It is clear that the nineteenth century laid the foundations for the Mexico and the Mexican-Americans of today.

1

Down from Colonialism: Mexico's Nineteenth-Century Crisis*

Jaime E. Rodríguez O.

Colonial Mexico (New Spain) was a vast territory characterized by a stable and responsive government, a wealthy and balanced economy, and a multi-racial society which enjoyed considerable social mobility. Yet, by the middle of the nineteenth century, the Republic of Mexico not only had lost more than half its territory, but also suffered from extreme political instability, severe economic depression, and both racial and class conflict. This essay will examine Mexico's decline from colonial well-being to republican disaster. Since many people today mistakenly consider the colonial era to have been backward, feudal, and exploitative, I shall begin by contrasting New Spain in 1800 with Mexico around 1850.

The Viceroyalty of New Spain was the Western Hemisphere's most imposing political structure at the end of the eighteenth century. Its territory included present-day Mexico, Central America, the Philippines, Cuba, Puerto Rico, Florida, the coastal regions of Alabama and Mississippi, and all the lands west of the Mississippi River, as well as claims to western Canada and Alaska. The heartland of the viceroyalty, however, was a region about the size of present-day Mexico, known as the Kingdom of New Spain. That area, the subject of this essay, was the richest and most populous part of the viceroyalty. New Spain's institutions responded well to local needs. Indeed, a notable feature of the colony's government was its legitimacy, derived from the confidence it engendered in all classes and races. Colonial Mexicans normally availed themselves of administrative and legal procedures to obtain relief. Even Indians had sufficient confidence in the legal system to seek redress in the courts where they frequently won their suits, because colonial tribunals recognized the validity of native laws and customs. Thus, there was general agreement in New Spain that royal government, both at the local and the imperial level, served the public interest. This consensus did not mean that all disputes were settled peacefully; violence occasionally erupted. But such outbursts were rare, seeking to remedy specific grievances, not to challenge the colony's political, social, or economic order. To a great extent, this success was due to the fact that New Spain drew upon its domestic elite for guidance. Colonial Mexicans generally responded to their country's problems with moderate, rational, and practical solutions.

The colony's great wealth contributed to government stability and to the dynamism of Mexican society. New Spain provided two-thirds of the revenue of the Spanish empire. In 1799, this amounted to 20 million pesos, 10 million of which was spent for local administration and defense; 4 million subsidized other areas of the viceroyalty in Central and North America, the Caribbean, and the Philippines; and 6 million was remitted to the royal treasury in Madrid. Revenues increased during the next decade, averaging 24 million pesos per year. In 1806, when unusual demands were placed on the Spanish colonies, Mexico raised 39 million pesos, sending 19 million to Spain to help finance the wars in Europe.[1]

The economy of New Spain was healthy, balanced, and, for the most part, functioned independently of the mother country. Although precious metals represented 84 percent of all exports, the colony did not become a simple monoproducer, as some dependency theorists have suggested. Despite its critical and dynamic character, mining constituted only a minor portion of the colonial economy. In 1800, mining contributed 27.95 million pesos, or 13 percent of Mexico's annual production, while manufacturing accounted for 55 million, or 25 percent, and agriculture 138.63 million, or 62 percent. Mexico's large and diversified internal market consumed 86 percent of all national production, as table 1 shows.

The silver mines, however, served as engines of economic growth, encouraging the expansion of agriculture, commerce, and manufacturing. Mexico was the world's principal supplier of silver throughout the colonial period. During the years 1780–1810, New Spain produced an average of 24 million pesos of silver annually.[2] Although precise figures on production are not available, one can estimate silver output by examining coinage, which accounted for more than 95% of the silver mined in Mexico.

Mining required investments on a vast scale. The cost of labor, machinery, and supplies necessary for the largest operations was stag-

TABLE 1

Estimates (in pesos) of New Spain's Gross National Product ca. 1800

Sector	Domestic Consumption Amount	%	Exports Amount	%	Total Amount	%
Agriculture	133,782,625	70.5	4,844,685	15.1	138,627,310	62.0
Industry	54,744,047	29.0	257,264	0.8	55,001,311	25.0
Mining	924,259	0.5	27,026,741	84.1	27,951,000	13.0
Total	189,450,931	100.0	32,128,690	100.0	221,579,621	100.0
% of the Economy	86		14		100	

Source: Calculated from José María Quirós, *Memoria de estatuto* (Veracruz, 1817). Errors in the figures originally published by Quirós have been corrected by Doris M. Ladd, *The Mexican Nobility at Independence* (Austin: Institute of Latin American Studies, U. of Texas, 1976) 26.

gering. In the 1780s for example, Antonio de Obregón borrowed capital from local merchants to rework old sixteenth-century diggings in Guanajuato. After spending over 2 million pesos to sink some of the deepest mine shafts in existence, his mines produced silver valued at 30.9 million pesos from 1788 to 1809. In just one year, 1791, his mine yielded as much silver as the entire Viceroyalty of Peru.[3] When considering the magnitude of the sums involved in this venture, one should keep in mind that in 1800, the per capita income of England, the most advanced nation in the world, equalled 196 pesos a year.[4] Obregón's impressive achievement depended entirely on local resources. In studying this and other eighteenth-century Mexican ventures, one is struck by the high level of capital formation, technological innovation, entrepreneurial spirit, and managerial skills possessed by Mexicans.

A brief comparison with the United States highlights the nature of Mexico's economy in 1800. The per capita income for New Spain was about 116 pesos a year compared with 165 pesos for the United States. The value of Mexican and United States' exports was the same, about 20 million pesos.[5] Both countries were predominantly agricultural, but Mexico possessed a much larger industrial sector, principally in mining and textile manufacturing.

Other aspects of life in the neighboring regions provide an interesting contrast. In 1800, the United States had a population of 6 million people while Mexico's inhabitants numbered about 4 million. The United States was overwhelmingly rural, while Mexico, although rural,

TABLE 2

Coinage of Silver in Mexico, 1796–1825

Year	Millions of Pesos	Year	Millions of Pesos
1796[a]	24.4	1811[c,e]	10.1
1797[a]	24.1	1812[c,e]	7.7
1798[a]	23.0	1813[c,e]	9.8
1799[a]	21.1	1814[d,e]	10.1
1800[a]	17.9	1815[d,e]	8.3
1801[a]	16.0	1816[c,e]	9.6
1802[a]	18.0	1817[c,e]	9.1
1803[a]	22.5	1818[d,e]	12.6
1804[a]	26.1	1819[c]	12.8
1805[a]	25.8	1820[c]	10.8
1806[a]	23.4	1821[d,e]	7.6
1807[a]	20.7	1822[d]	10.4
1808[a]	20.5	1823[d]	10.8
1809[a]	24.7	1824[d]	9.0
1810[b]	18.0	1825[d]	8.3

[a] Mint of Mexico.
[b] Mints of Mexico and Zacatecas.
[c] Mints of Mexico, Zacatecas, and Durango.
[d] Mints of Mexico, Zacatecas, Durango, and Guadalajara.
[e] During the war years, the mints of Guadalajara and Durango failed to make annual reports, but instead reported for periods of time varying from 6 to 45 months. Since it was impossible to disaggregate those numbers, monthly averages were calculated and multiplied by 12 to obtain yearly figures. Although this approach introduces a degree of error, the figures presented in the table are sound estimates of silver coinage for the period.

Source: Calculated from the annual reports of the mints of Mexico City, Guadalajara, Durango, and Zacatecas which are reproduced in Ward, *Mexico* 1: 386–91.

had several of the largest cities on the continent. The principal urban centers of the United States—New York with 60,000 people, Philadelphia with 41,000, and Boston with 25,000—did not compare with the leading cities in New Spain—Mexico City with 150,000 inhabitants, Guanajuato with 60,000, Querétaro with 50,000, Puebla with 40,000, and Zacatecas with 30,000. Colonial Mexico also differed from the United States in its racial composition and in the greater degree of mobility enjoyed by its people. Europeans constituted the majority of the United States' population, with blacks and Indians forming significant minorities. Whites, however, dominated the political and economic structure of the country, limiting social mobility to members of their race. In contrast, the Mexican census of 1793 indicated that there were approximately 8,000 Europeans, that is, persons born in the Old World; about 700,000 *criollos* — a group considered white but which, in fact, included a majority of people of mixed ancestry who claimed white status by virtue of education and wealth; some 420,000 *mestizos* — individuals of mixed Indian and Spanish origin, but also including acculturated Indians who passed for mestizos; 360,000 *mulatos*; 6,000 blacks; and 2,300,000 Indians.[6] The Indian enumeration includes more than a million who were acculturated and who could, in essence, be considered mestizos. Unfortunately for the historian, the census failed to enumerate Asians, making it impossible to know their true numbers. Perhaps 100,000 Asians immigrated to Mexico during the colonial period. By 1800 they, like the countless Africans brought to the colony, had entered the racially mixed population. Thus Mexico, unlike its northern counterpart, had a multiracial society integrated through miscegenation.

Economic, not racial, factors constituted the main determinants of social status. While colonial Mexicans regarded being white as a positive characteristic, the records of New Spain provide numerous examples of upwardly mobile people of color who attained elite status by making money and then claiming to be white. Indeed, in the eighteenth century, there were so many claimants to white status that in return for a sum of money, the king granted his American subjects a certificate of whiteness, a *Cédula de Gracias al sacar*. But in New Spain, it was better to be rich than white; rich mestizos and mulattos often hired poor white immigrants from Spain as servants.[7]

Eighteenth-century Mexico can be described as a wealthy, capitalist society whose economy was characterized by private ownership of the means of production; by profit-oriented entrepreneurs; by a free-wage labor force; and by the exchange of capital, labor, goods, and services in a free market. While there were some limits on the mobility of these economic factors, present research indicates that these restrictions posed no greater obstacles than those existing in eighteenth-century England and the United States.

The contrast between New Spain and republican Mexico in 1850 was enormous. The wars of independence and the chaos that followed ruined the nation's economy and destroyed the legitimacy of its institutions. Between 1821 and 1850, only one president, Guadalupe Victoria (1824–1828), completed his term of office. His success is primarily attributable to the two large foreign loans negotiated in 1824 and 1825 which gave his administration financial latitude. During the next twenty years, the Republic endured three constitutions, twenty governments, and more than one hundred cabinets. As succeeding administrations proved unable to maintain order and protect lives and property, the country sank into anarchy. Fear and uncertainty became commonplace. Ex-soldiers-turned-bandits infested the highways, obstructing commerce and threatening small towns. These, and other manifestations of social dissolution, contributed to Mexico's instability. The situation worsened when political conflict degenerated into civil war in 1834. Large sections of the country were ravaged as federalists and centralists, liberals and conservatives fought for political control. During 1835–1845, secessionists established the republics of Yucatán, Texas, and the Rio Grande, but only Texas managed to consolidate its independence. The other regions, however, maintained their autonomy, if not their independence, from the national government by force of arms.[8]

The country's political instability made Mexico easy prey to foreign aggressors. The Republic endured invasions by Spain in 1829; France in 1838; the United States in 1847; and England, Spain, and France in 1861. The nation's disintegration prompted foreign exponents of racial superiority, among them Karl Marx, to hope that "the energetic Yankees" would overwhelm and replace the "lazy" and "degenerate" Mexicans who were incapable of progress.[9] By 1850, many Mexicans feared that their nation would cease to exist; the country had lost more that half its territory and national regeneration seemed unattainable.

During these years, government revenue dropped from an 1806 high of 39 million pesos to a low of 5.4 million in 1823. In the last two decades of the colonial period, government income had averaged 24 million pesos annually, compared to 12.2 million in the Republic's first decade. The average annual revenue increased from 1834 to 1844 to 23 million pesos, but not until the 1880s did collections surpass late colonial averages. The decline in government income reflected Mexico's postindependence economic depression. Mining provides a graphic example of this crisis. Mineral production fell from an annual average of 25 million pesos in the late colonial period to a low of 6.5 million in 1819, averaging 11 million a year for the next four decades. This dramatic decline was due to decreased production, not to a drop in the price of silver. From 1801 to 1810, New Spain extracted 5.5 million kilograms, while from 1821 to 1830, Mexican silver production had fallen to 2.6 million kilograms.[10] Silver output did not equal late colonial production averages until the 1880s. Other sectors ex-

TABLE 3

Government Revenue for Selected Years, 1823–1850

Year[1]	Income[2]	Year[1]	Income[2]
1823	5,409,722	1836	26,478,509
1824	8,452,828	1837	18,477,979
1825[a]	9,720,771	1838	15,037,038
1826[b]	13,848,257	1839	27,518,577
1827	14,192,132	1840	19,858,472
1828	11,640,737	1841	21,273,477
1829	12,815,009	1842	26,683,696
1830	12,200,020	1843	29,323,423
1831	17,256,882	1844	25,905,348
1832	16,375,960	1849[c]	23,460,820
1834	19,798,464	1850	16,765,762

[1] Year runs from July through June unless noted. For example, 1827 included income for period July 1826–June 1827.
[2] Net income in pesos.
[a] January 1825–August 1825.
[b] September 1825–June 1826.
[c] January 1848–June 1849.

Source: These figures were calculated from data in the reports of the Minister of Treasury. Secretaria de Hacienda, *Memoria* (México, 1823–50).

TABLE 4

Mexican Silver Production, 1825–1849

Years	Five year annual average in millions of pesos
1825–29	9.2
1830–34	11.3
1835–39	11.5
1840–44	12.4
1845–49	15.6

Sources: Calculated from A. Soetbeer, *Edelmetall-produktion un werthverhältniss zwishen gold und silver* (Gotha, 1874) 55; Miguel Lerdo de Tejada, *Comercio exterior de México desde la Conquista hasta hoy*, 2nd ed. (México: Banco Nacional de Comercio Exterior, 1967).

perienced similar dislocations. Exports fell from 20 million pesos in 1800 to 5 million in 1825, and averaged 9.5 million for the next three decades.[11]

While Mexico declined and then stagnated, the United States and Western Europe experienced rapid population increase and economic growth. In 1800, New Spain, like the United States, had a dynamic, expanding economy, but during the next fifty years, Mexico fell dramatically behind. The Republic grew to 8 million while the population of the United States expanded to 23 million. Mexico's annual per capita income fell from 116 pesos at the end of the colonial period to 56 pesos in 1845, while U.S. per capita income more than doubled. Thus, Mexicans who had earned 70 percent of U.S. per capita income in 1800 were reduced to 14 percent in 1845. Even more significant, Mexican output which had equaled 51 percent of U.S. GNP in 1800, declined to only 8 percent in 1845.[12] In contrast to the capitalist, market-oriented, free-wage labor economy of the eighteenth century, mid-nineteenth-century Mexico must be characterized as having a dual economy. A market-oriented sector remained, but it encompassed only some areas, such as Mexico City and the few remaining large provincial cities. Most of the country had retreated into self-sufficiency.[13] Ironically, Mexico in 1850 possessed the sort of society and economy which many today mistakenly believe to have characterized colonial Mexico.

The startling contrast between colonial prosperity and order, and republican poverty and disorder defies easy explanations. It is a paradox which can be understood if one realizes that New Spain developed a costly and complex, but extremely fragile, infrastructure in a land that is both poor and harsh. Mexico, a country with limited natural resources, has considerable natural obstacles to national development and integration. Climatic variations that bridge the extremes of stifling heat on the coast and the chilling cold of the mountains pose a severe threat to people and crops. The northern third of the nation is a desert while rain forests cover large areas of the south. Fifty percent of Mexico suffers from a perpetual scarcity of water; only thirteen percent of the country enjoys sufficient rainfall to sustain crops without irrigation. The richest soil often lacks water. Most of the countryside must cope with intermittent drought followed by torrential rains which destroy rather than nourish the land. Less than ten percent of Mexico is arable without extensive man-made improvements. But even with such improvements, the arable soil increases to only about 15 percent of the nation's territory, an area equal to the arable land in the state of Kansas.[14] Thus, Mexico is impoverished in the most important resource known to man, agricultural land.

Topography is a major barrier to the use of the nation's limited natural resources. Great mountain ranges dominate the landscape. Deep gorges and huge canyons scar Mexico, isolating some of its most productive lands in high mountain valleys. Since the country has no navigable rivers, transportation and communication are restricted to land routes, which are universally expensive when compared to water transport. It was prohibitive in Mexico, as elsewhere, to move cheap bulky products long distances overland. The country's rugged topography, which increased the difficulty and cost of building and maintaining land routes, magnified this general limitation to interregional exchanges. Since many of the roads passed through mountainous terrain and were subject to destruction by floods, earthquakes, and volcanic eruptions, the nation's communications network required unusually high maintenance costs.[15] It was, moreover, a fragile system that, once constructed, required constant upkeep.

The wars of independence severely damaged agriculture, commerce, industry, and mining, as well as the nation's complex but delicate infrastructure. Lamentably, the most serious fighting occurred in central Mexico, the richest agricultural and mining area of the country. Rebels burned farms, killed livestock, wrecked mining equipment, and paralyzed commerce. Royalist forces retaliated with counter-terror, devastating regions which had capitulated to or supported the insurgents. The viceregal government lost control of most of the country to rebel bands or to royalist military leaders who acted without regard for law or the needs of the economy. By 1821, when Mexico achieved independence, the nation was in chaos and the economy in ruins.[16] Although it is impossible to assess the full impact of the struggle for independence, contemporaries attempted to calculate the magnitude of the destruction. José María Luis Mora believed that about 600,000 people—more than one-tenth of the population— perished from war, disease, and famine between 1810 and 1816, the period of heaviest fighting.[17] Quirós provides the best estimates of the losses caused by the war. He, like others, maintains that agriculture suffered great damage. But as he demonstrates, the most severe blow to the Mexican economy was the loss of capital; money either fled the country or was withdrawn from circulation.

Why did Mexico not recover soon after independence? Why did it sink into fifty years of economic depression and political turmoil? The answer is both economic and psychological. The economy was

TABLE 5

Estimates (in pesos) of Damage
Caused by Wars of Independence, 1810–1816

Loss to Agriculture	70,000,000
Loss to Mining	20,000,000
Loss to Industry	11,818,000
Loss in Currency (mostly silver)	786,000,000

Source: Calculated from José María Quirós, *Memoria de estatuto* (Veracruz, 1817).

in ruins as a result of the wars of independence and, especially, as a result of the postindependence political chaos. But in addition, Mexicans lost confidence in their country's institutions. They either exported their capital or withdrew it from circulation. This, along with the collapse of the nation's credit system, led to a massive contraction of investment. Although Mexico obtained foreign loans and investments in the postindependence period, these were insufficient to compensate for the great loss of national capital.

Contemporary observers provide us with graphic accounts of postindependence conditions. In 1822, Joel Poinsett, the first United States minister to Mexico, noted the destruction of many haciendas and the great financial loss such devastation represented to agriculturalists. He depicted San Felipe, Guanajuato, a once-prosperous farming and mining center, as representing

> another example of the horrors of civil war. Scarcely a house was entire; and except for one church lately rebuilt, the town appeared to be in ruins. We stopped in the principal square, and passed through arches built of porphyry into a courtyard of a building which had once been magnificent; nothing but the porticos and the ground floor remain.[18]

The English traveler G. F. Lyon described the situation on the road between the once-rich cities of San Luis Potosí and Zacatecas as follows:

> The prosperity of this place [an hacienda] is attributed to the owner having armed his people in defense of this property during the devastating Revolutionary War; and its contrast with Ranchos [middle sized farms] which we had passed on our day's ride was very striking. There we saw the houses roofless and in ruins blackened by fire, and had ridden over plains still bearing the faint trace of the plow; but the Rancheros who had tilled this ground had been murdered with their whole families during the war.[19]

All published travel accounts report similar devastation. Perhaps the great silver mining region of Guanajuato demonstrates most accurately postwar Mexico's changed conditions. During 1801-1809, its mines produced silver worth 47 million pesos, but yielded only 22 million in the following decade.[20] In 1820, the flooding of Valenciana, the greatest silver mine in the world, proved catastrophic because, as the Ayuntamiento observed,

> Valenciana, the incomparable Valenciana . . . the only mine that has for some time continued to support almost all our population, though with hardship, will be utterly stopped . . . It is believed that the remains of what used to be our numerous population will now flee the city to emigrate, to seek sustenance somewhere else, for here, when the mines and refineries do not function there is absolutely nothing to do. The prime harvests that the bounty of this year promises will not aid Guanajuato for there will be no one to buy and no money to buy it with.[21]

Apparently, the city council's assessment proved quite accurate because travelers subsequently described the city as desolate, filled with unemployed, poverty-stricken people who huddled in misery in the remains of ruined buildings.

Even the great metropolis, Mexico City, seems to have lost population. Many of those who remained suffered from unemployment or severe underemployment. Visitors left vivid accounts of these poor wretches, whom they called *léperos* because of their filthy, tattered clothes.[22] All reports indicate that the work force had severely contracted. Thousands of miners, textile workers, artisans, muleteers, carters, and other skilled workers lost their jobs.

The destruction of the silver mines during the wars of independence and the chaos that followed were, perhaps, the most important factors in Mexico's economic depression. The speedy rehabilitation of the mining sector would have immensely aided national recovery, but the problems associated with reviving the mines proved insurmountable. The combatants destroyed expensive machinery that was difficult to replace. Equipment that escaped vandalism was often neglected, allowed to rust, or otherwise deteriorate. The fighting interdicted supplies required by the mining centers. Without those supplies, the mines could not function. They consumed thousands of hides, since leather was used to make many things that are today manufactured from rubber or plastic, such as impermeable containers, belts, and gaskets. The mines also used large quantities of other materials, like grain to feed workers and draft animals; hemp for ropes, bags, and other equipment; carts and mules for transport; and cloth. The suspension of mining operations often resulted in severe damage to the mines themselves. Mexico's richest mines extracted ore from the world's deepest mine shafts. Left unattended, these deep tunnels rapidly flooded with ground water seepage, or, as in the case of Valenciana, heavy rains. Eventually, the flooding weakened the timbers and other supports, causing the tunnels to collapse. Once cave-ins occurred, it became tremendously expensive to reopen the mines.[23]

Two additional factors affected the recovery of the mines: mercury supplies and finances. Mexico's silver mines relied primarily on the patio or amalgamation process for separating silver from the ore. This technique required large quantities of mercury. At the onset of the nineteenth century, there were only three important sources of mercury: the Huancavelica mine in Peru, the Adria mine in present-day Yugoslavia, and the Almadén mine in Spain. The output of the Huancavelica mercury mine had declined and, after independence, could satisfy only Peruvian needs. International politics curtailed Mexican access to mercury from European mines: the Austrian empire, an ally of Spain, controlled Adria. Spain's Almadén mercury mine refused to supply Mexico until after 1838, when the two nations established diplomatic relations. Though Mexican miners could purchase quicksilver through intermediaries, the supplies were never certain. The cost of mercury increased dramatically, not only because of its scarcity, but also because Spain had subsidized silver mining by providing mercury to Mexican miners at cost. In an independent Mexico, mine owners had to pay prevailing market prices for mercury.

Finances, however, were the greatest obstacle to the recovery of mining. In the colonial period, Mexican entrepreneurs had raised millions of pesos from local sources to finance mining operations. The war and the unstable conditions that followed destroyed the public confidence necessary for investment. Mexicans and foreigners alike agreed that the collapse of the country's investment and credit system prevented recovery.[24] Unable to raise the necessary quantities of money internally, Mexican miners formed joint stock companies to attract foreign capital to Mexico. The English invested heavily in silver mines and frequently became the major stockholders of Mexican mines. But the cost of rebuilding Mexican silver mines proved to be so great that the British silver mining ventures were bankrupt by the middle of the nineteenth century.[25] Mexicans subsequently benefitted from these investments; when mining recovered in the 1880s, nationals had regained control of the industry.

The textile industry, like silver mining, proved difficult to revive after independence. Woolen and cotton textile production had been the largest and most important manufacturing enterprise in colonial Mexico. *Obrajes,* large-scale factories employing several hundred workers, were common in central Mexico, principally Querétaro, Puebla, and Mexico City. Indian villages often engaged in large-scale textile production in community-run obrajes. There were also many individuals operating small firms with one or two looms. In the eighteenth century, these small enterprises manufactured more than one-third of New Spain's woolen cloth. The wars of independence and the chaos that followed crippled the industry. Many obrajes were destroyed, and those which survived encountered difficulty in obtaining raw materials and distributing their finished products because transportation networks were disrupted. In addition, for a few years in the 1820s, Europeans flooded the Mexican market with cheap textiles, thus reducing the demand for local products.

After independence, the Mexican government tried to rehabilitate the textile industry by imposing high tariffs and financing the modernization of the industry. Although tariff barriers substantially reduced the influx of foreign textiles, the Mexican factories recovered slowly. The greatest obstacle was the shortage of capital. To overcome this deficiency, the Mexican government founded a development bank, the Banco de Avío, in 1830 which, unfortunately, did not possess sufficient resources to stimulate a rapid recovery. Government reports indicate that by 1846, the Banco de Avío had contributed less than ten percent of the ten million pesos which industrialists had invested in the textile industry. Puebla was the principal beneficiary of this investment. The city was well located to benefit from the stimulus because of its proximity to the large Mexico City market and to the port of Veracruz, which facilitated the importation of equipment. By the mid-nineteenth century, textiles, primarily cotton, reemerged as an important industry in Puebla, but total Mexican production still did not equal the average of late colonial output until the 1880s.[26]

Agriculture, which employed the overwhelming majority of Mexicans, could not escape the dislocations that beset the industrial sector. Government reports, travel accounts, and private correspondence indicate the wretched condition of commercial agriculture. Small farmers appear to have suffered most. Many were driven from their lands, first by the war and then by the violence, political chaos, and economic decline that followed. Since small farmers were the backbone of Mexican agriculture, their plight had severe repercussions.[27] Farmers lost their markets when the mines collapsed and urban centers contracted. Many Indian villages, which had once produced for the market, withdrew into subsistence agriculture. In the colonial period, large numbers of Indian communities specialized in growing wheat for the urban markets or the mines; others devoted their efforts to raising mules for transport and for heavy work in mines and factories. In 1800, villages raised millions of mules; by 1850, the number had fallen to thousands. Depressed demand for agricultural products resulted in the abandonment of large tracts of land which formerly had been cultivated. Irrigation systems decayed, while livestock depleted the soil by overgrazing.

Mexico City, and a few other large population centers, continued to demand agricultural products from the countryside, but after independence, they curtailed imports from distant regions; local production sufficed for their needs. Many large estates went bankrupt or were abandoned. As in the case of mining, Mexicans encouraged foreigners to invest in agriculture. Europeans purchased large estates in the early 1820s, but they also lost money. By the middle of the nineteenth century, European investors had relinquished their Mexican holdings. The small farmers, who managed to remain on the land, enjoyed a degree of prosperity because they could control their overhead more easily than the large *hacendados*.[28] Agriculture, like the rest of the economy, would not fully recover until the 1880s.

The slump in the mines limited the performance of Mexico's export sector in the postindependence period, since silver remained the country's principal export; as mining declined, the nation's exports fell. Export substitution, given existing technology, was impossible; Mexico's high transportation costs prevented the export of bulky agricultural products at competitive prices. Because its excellent network of rivers permitted the shipment of these products at low cost, the United States, in contrast, exported a variety of agricultural commodities. Mexico's foreign trade stagnated at a time of massive and rapid expansion of world trade. By 1850, United States exports were twenty times greater than those of Mexico. Indeed, by the 1880s, when the silver mines recovered sufficiently to equal late colonial levels, the pattern of world trade had changed, and new and significant silver producers had emerged, among them the United Stats. In 1800, Mexico had produced 75 percent of the world's silver; by 1880, its output represented less than 40 percent.[29]

Mexico required massive investment simply to restore it to the preindependence level of production, but, unfortunately, the nation's credit system proved unequal to the task. Because Spain failed to develop modern financial institutions, such as banks and commercial houses, colonial Mexicans relied on two principal sources of credit: personal loans and the Church. While personal loans from wealthy families or entrepreneurs were common throughout the colonial period, the Church served as New Spain's principal banker. Convents, nunneries, schools, orphanages, and hospitals often received dowries, endowments, and bequests, which they invested in order to earn regular income. Generally, religious corporations loaned these funds to property owners, who paid an annuity. Each diocese also had a *Juzgado de Testamentos, Capellanías y Obras Pías* (Court of Testaments, Chantries, and Pious Works) which administered the endowments entrusted to the tribunal by the faithful. (A capellanía was a benefice for a chaplain who was required to say Masses for the soul of the benefactor, and a pious work could be any sort of charity.) The juzgados invested these sums by lending primarily to land owners. As was the case with credit extended by other church bodies, the juzgados sought to earn a return of five to six percent on the capital so that the chaplain of the philanthropy would enjoy a regular income. Over the years, religious corporations invested vast sums of money in the economy of New Spain.[30]

Small farmers and Indian villagers who either did not possess adequate collateral or who were unwilling to mortgage their lands often turned to the *repartimiento de comercio,* an informal system through which provincial officials distributed seed, tools, and other agricultural necessities on credit. These magistrates often facilitated the purchase or sale of livestock, and marketed products for groups who might not have otherwise found outlets for their commodities. The officials were able to provide credit because they established commercial ties with wealthy entrepreneurs. The repartimiento system offered opportunities for abuse, since magistrates sometimes used their authority to force Indian communities and small farmers to buy items they did not need or to sell their products at lower than market prices. Despite occasional irregularities, the repartimiento de comercio functioned reasonably well as a system of rural credit.[31]

Mexico's credit structure came under attack even before the wars of independence. Eighteenth-century enlightened Spanish reformers criticized what they considered to be the evils of the repartimiento de comercio and the system of Church credit. In the 1790s, they convinced the crown to abolish the repartimiento de comercio, contending that it exploited Indian communities. Then in 1804, the colonial credit structure suffered a crippling blow when the crown ordered the confiscation of Church wealth to prosecute the war in Europe. Between 1804 and 1808, Church bodies had to foreclose on loans totaling 44 million pesos, 12 million of which they remitted to Spain. The assaults on Mexico's credit structure debilitated the economy and fomented the discontent which eventually culminated in the movement for independence.[32]

While the wars of emancipation aggravated Mexico's already weakened credit system, the instability and chaos that followed engendered a severe loss of confidence. As a result, wealthy entrepreneurs refused to extend credit to individuals, preferring instead to lend for a short term, at exorbitant rates, to the government. The practice continued after 1821 because the national government could not raise sufficient revenue through taxation. The entrepreneurs-turned-loan sharks justified their actions, arguing that other investments were unsafe and that the high interest they demanded was reasonable because governments, which often failed to pay their debts, were poor credit risks. The nation's financial crisis worsened because religious corporations began to lend large sums only to individuals or groups who were proclerical. This policy seemed warranted, in their view, because Spanish reformers had expropriated Church wealth at the end of the colonial period and liberal republican governments continued to threaten their holdings after independence.

As a result of these events, the credit system which had served New Spain well for nearly 300 years virtually ceased to function after independence. Mexico's government and entrepreneurs increasingly had to turn to foreign credit sources. Although foreigners, mostly the English, did invest large sums in Mexico, the amount did not satisfy the country's needs. Mexico did not develop an adequate banking and credit system until the 1880s.

The process of national recovery required more than sixty years. Unfortunately for Mexico, drastic changes transformed the world economic system during those decades. The Industrial Revolution altered the north Atlantic. In 1800, the United States was a second-rank agrarian nation while western Europe was only beginning to industrialize. Many contemporaries, among them Alexander von Humboldt, believed not only that Mexico could compete successfully for economic hegemony, but that it would emerge as the colossus of the American continent.[33] No one had such illusions in 1880. The United States was an emerging industrial power; western European industrial corporations and financial institutions had achieved such size and strength that nascent Mexican enterprises could not compete with them. After 1876, the leaders of a recently unified Mexico, therefore, decided to exchange economic independence for external assistance in industrial and financial development. Although this step led to rapid industrialization and modernization, it placed the control of Mexican development in the hands of foreigners. The violent Revolution of 1910 rejected that accommodation. Since 1910, Mexican governments have balanced the desire for national economic sovereignty with the need for foreign capital and technology. One can only speculate how Mexico might have developed without the nineteenth-century crisis.

2

Where Did All the Royalists Go? New Light on the Military Collapse of New Spain, 1810–1822

Christon I. Archer

To read the documents of late colonial Bourbon Mexico, it is difficult to predict the upheaval that occurred with cataclysmic force beginning in 1810 with the Revolt of Padre Miguel Hidalgo. There were signs of discontent manifested in rivalries between the peninsular and creole elites and from the dispossessed *castas* that suffered most from economic cycles, regional crop failures, and administrative alterations. To an increasing degree, outside influences such as international wars and new philosophies had begun to touch Mexico. However, there did not appear to be any sector or mechanism in New Spain that was capable of breaking the solid grip of the regime and of the ruling minority. Fear of unleashing the Indian-mestizo majority made most Mexican creoles balk at the prospect of revolution along the lines of the Anglo-American experience.

Until it was knocked off balance by a complex series of internal and external forces, the Spanish regime continued in power through tradition and inertia. Hidalgo, José María Morelos, and many other less well known insurgent leaders who emerged in or after 1810 were the catalysts who exposed the political and socio-economic iniquities of the old regime and pushed it until finally it crumbled. Once violence replaced obedience, the desire for independence became an unquenchable force. The royalists might regain control of rebel territory and convince themselves that they were winning, but there were new insurgents ready to join the old ones in a struggle that had local and regional connotations as well as the goal of national independence.

Charisma was insufficient in itself for Hidalgo to raise and then maintain a massive force composed mostly of Indians and castas dedicated to the definitive destruction of the hated *gachupines* (European Spaniards). Certainly his somewhat mystical program of revolution, religion, and reform struck a responsive chord among these sectors. There was much more to Hidalgo's army than a mob of frenzied Indians whose major goal was booty, pillage, and the overthrow of the ruling elite. To the shock of the royalist regime, support for Spain in the Bajío region and in some other parts of Mexico rested in an isolated minority that often lacked meaningful ties with the great mass of the population.

The successes of Hidalgo and his leadership lay in unifying a potential infrastructure of local chiefs who existed beneath or parallel with the official regime of *subdelegados* and local representatives of viceregal or Church power. The devouring mob portrayed by royalist commanders was only one element of the picture. Out of old networks of local ties and traditional loyalties, the insurgents patched together a fairly effective system of resistance. Hacienda mayordomos, innkeepers, *arrieros,* lower rank militia officers and NCOs, village and town priests, and others who possessed links with the populace through a web of business and social connections came forward to embrace the cause of independence. Although most district or regional leaders had very little theoretical knowledge about revolutions or political organizations, they offered the prospect of something better. Their messages concerned the availability of land owned by absentee owners, the opportunity to share in the riches of New Spain, the removal of an oppressive social and economic system, and an end to different local grievances caused by overbearing or corrupt officials, unpopular taxes, and other special regional situations.

While the royalist army was able to regain the initiative against the poorly armed and trained forces of Hidalgo and Morelos, most officers expressed shock at the lack of support accorded to the Spanish cause. Félix Calleja, commander of the Army of the Center, described the general population as ". . . immoral, without character, and lacking customs." Like so many of his associates from 1810 to 1821, Calleja felt isolated and somewhat intimidated in a country populated by a hostile majority. The insurgents soon learned that they could not challenge disciplined army units on the conventional field of battle, but this did not alter their deeply rooted animosities toward the Spanish ruling class.[1] While Mexicans gave an outward impression of loyalty when royalist troops were present in force, they returned to insurrection using guerrilla warfare as soon as the army was out of the way. In many provinces, the restoration of royalist control was made more difficult because there were few trustworthy people available to head a royalist administration. This meant the importation of outside officials, and very often new grievances caused by arbitrary or corrupt rule. Calleja believed that eighty percent of the population desired an insurgent victory.[2] If this statistical imbalance against the royalist cause did not discourage army officers, knowledge about Spanish unpopularity sapped morale over time and made for policies that could not be sustained forever. Terror of army retribution restored sullen acquiescence, but soldiers knew that "in their hearts they (the Mexicans) abhor the Europeans."[3]

The focus of insurgent hatred upon the gachupines and their centuries of oppression demoralized the peninsulares and the pro-European creole minorities that should have taken the lead in supporting the royalist cause. During the first phases of the revolution, fear of rebel victory drove Europeans and wealthy creoles out of their regional towns and provinces into the major cities which became the objects of blockades and sieges. Rumors and horror stories detailing abominable atrocities created an atmosphere of terror that bred defeatism. The flight of merchants, landowners, and administrators in search of safety weakened regional defenses and encouraged many of their former subordinates to adopt neutrality or to move directly into the insurgent camp.[4] The loss of bureaucrats, technicians, merchants, miners, senior prelates, and other essential personnel left some provinces close to anarchy. Those who fled transmitted panic to areas untouched by the revolt. The desire to resist insurrection evaporated.[5] Even the army commanders became preoccupied by the thought of a general collapse that would leave the royalists without Mexican territory to defend.[6]

During late 1810 and early 1811, the Europeans and creoles had good reason to be frightened. Gachupín prisoners were marched in the vanguard of Hidalgo's forces and messages were sent in advance that any resistance would provoke mass executions.[7] At Zapotlán el Grande, the Indian residents rose up spontaneously and, without regard to origins, slaughtered all Europeans and creoles. More than 600 European Spaniards perished at Guanajuato and another 130 were murdered in cold blood at San Felipe.[8] At the small Indian village of San Francisco, north of Mexico City, the inhabitants kept the bloody garments of executed gachupines as grisly trophies.[9] During Hidalgo's occupation of Valladolid (Morelia), small groups of European prisoners were marched out of the city daily to be executed by firing squads. Robbed of all possessions and reduced in some cases to begging for food, their wives and children were not even permitted to mourn the loss of their husbands and fathers.[10]

Whether it was a premeditated policy or simply the result of bitter hatred directed against the privileged minority, insurgent terror was a potent tool in melting the peninsular Spaniards' resolve to fight. And because the wealthy creole whites looked and acted the same as the gachupines, many of them feared for their lives and properties. Some Spaniards who had emigrated to Mexico to better their social and economic situations now sought to escape. As Europeans, they had insisted upon special privileges and made themselves into an easily identified target. Now they found themselves the focus of accumulated animosities — the lightning rod for insurgent fury. It is little wonder that increasing numbers chose flight over resistance; many gave up altogether on Mexico to seek refuge at Havana or to return to metropolitan Spain. To Félix Calleja, this was the coward's way out. While he recognized that Mexican hatred of gachupines was impossible to exterminate, he believed that vigorous counterinsurgency combined with military mobilization of the population and some reforms would restore the country to order. Instead of running, he wanted the Europeans to show their resolve by enlisting in the royalist army.[11]

For years Calleja complained that the European Spaniards were "pacific spectators" in a bloody war that designated them as a central factor. While loyal Mexican soldiers risked assassination on nocturnal patrols, death in skirmishes, and at least joined the royalist defense forces, the European Spaniards criticized the war effort and made even greater demands for special police and army protection. Many lived in luxury and occupied themselves with their own narrow interests. Calleja wanted them to enlist a special European militia unit that would accept men up to 60 years of age, but there were insufficient volunteers. Rather than inspiring the Mexicans with their tenacity and dedication, the Spaniards left the fighting and deprivations to the creoles. Calleja failed absolutely in his mission to raise an all-European force of 700 to 800 troops.[12]

The few peninsulares who did condescend to serve the royalist army followed past practices of their minority; they demanded special recognition, financial considerations, and military distinctions. Even if they lacked the most basic army training, they expected to commence service in high ranks and made other requests that jeopardized martial customs. In Calleja's opinion, most Europeans acted as if, by doing their duty to the king, they were awarding a grand favor to the nation and army.[13] He condemned their "lack of patriotism and criminal indifference" to the royalist cause.[14]

When he became viceroy in 1813, Calleja's reservations about the dedication of peninsular royalists increased. Now a resident in Mexico City, which was the haven for many provincial gachupín exiles, he wished to tap their manpower for the *cuerpos patrióticos* raised for police patrols and homefront defense. While many Mexico City residents were lukewarm about mobilizations, the peninsulares led in the evasion of enlistment. Many sought exemptions by producing licenses or passports authorizing resettlement or trips to Spain. On October 26, 1813, Calleja issued a *bando* prohibiting the use of travel documents to escape militia duty.[15] He stressed his opinion that any major exodus of wealthy Spaniards would damage Mexican industry, drain essential capital out of the wartorn country, and convey a very poor impression to the populace about the solidity of Spanish rule. As might be expected, European Spaniards resented controls that interfered with their liberties of movement. Calleja obtained support for his policy from the Audiencia of Mexico, but by July 1814, the imperial government overturned his general restrictions.[16]

The continued population outflow and accompanying drain of liquid capital essential to economic recovery returned Calleja to the problem. He published a new bando on February 9, 1815, restricting emigration from New Spain to persons who could certify a medical cause. In Calleja's view, the flight of honorable and wealthy persons "is the most regrettable blow in the present circumstances that the kingdom could suffer."[17] Loss of population and wealth deprived the regime of any opportunity to recover even if it won military victory over the insurgents. Not only was the country divided with much of the population anxious to achieve independence, but the erosion of the elite placed into question recovery plans for agriculture, mining, and industry. The disastrous downturn of commercial traffic and industrial output resulting from the war had increased dramatically the numbers of unemployed Mexicans who sought to improve their lot by joining the insurgent side. Calleja noted that rebel publications reported the high level of emigration and attributed it to the weakness of the Spanish regime and a prelude to the inevitable victory of independence.[18]

Wealthy Spaniards and creoles renewed their outcry, arguing that loyal subjects possessed the liberty to move families and property from the colony to the metropolis. On appeal, the Audiencia of Mexico upheld the petitions of those who wished to move without extraordinary regulations. While he continued to express fears about a debilitating general exodus, Calleja again lifted controls and agreed to concede passports to those who were eligible. Finally, the Council of the Indies examined the dispute and upheld the viceroy's right to deny petitions for travel to Iberia, depending upon the merits of individual cases and the general situation of the province. The Council recommended that equitable criteria be developed to avoid complaints from those who felt that they had not received fair treatment.[19]

To offset the civilian exodus from Mexico, from 1811 until the beginning of 1816 there was a significant inflow of European Spanish soldiers. These 12,000 to 15,000 peninsulares played a crucial role in improving the military prospects of the royalist cause, but at the same time their presence accelerated the erosion of essential royalist support. There can be no doubt that the Spanish battalions contributed to the military victory over the main force insurgent armies and then stiffened the creole army for years of counterinsurgency operations.

The *Regimientos de Infantería* of Lobera and América which arrived in New Spain in 1811 supported Calleja's creole Ejército del Centro during the difficult siege of Morelos's Cuautla de Amilpas. Until about 1818, the European *regimientos expedicionarios* were employed in a variety of sieges, operational situations, and garrisoned in unfriendly regions where their homogeneity added discipline to the less well trained provincial units that fought alongside them. The officers of these units and other Spanish officers who received transfers from Spain to Mexico helped to fill administrative positions abandoned earlier by the flight of civilian bureaucrats. These new officials militarized Mexico and added a martial flavor that was not appreciated by civilian intendants and other administrators. In their attitudes toward Mexicans, the new generation of army officeholders expressed many of the most negative opinions of previous generations of gachupín rulers. Indeed, the animosities and hatreds generated by the revolt made the army commanders even less capable of understanding the complexities of Mexico.

In many instances, Mexicans could not escape the old conclusions that Spaniards mined New Spain to retrieve lost fortunes, get rich quick, and then retire to the peninsula. Although Spanish army officers traditionally did not often volunteer for overseas postings, the French occupation of Spain caused many to lose their personal assets and left them without military offices at Cádiz. Initially, the Mexican insurgency appeared to offer the prospect of pay and career progression during a disastrous time in the metropolis. Significant numbers of intelligent, young officers with good connections, such as Brigadier José Moreno y Daoiz, who became commander of the important Puebla garrison, accepted transfer to Mexico.[20] However, after 1814 and the restoration of Fernando VII, some of these same officers reconsidered their moves and wished to rejoin the Spanish army so that they could retain crucial patronage links and personal contacts essential to the progress of their military careers. Moreover, a few years duty in Mexico made many officers realize that the nasty guerrilla war would neither be won quickly nor gain them much in the way of personal laurels. While combat offered opportunities for rapid promotions, most movement upward was below the rank of colonel and, even at that, the king had to sanction interim advances if they were to enhance future career opportunities in the metropolitan army. Given this situation, José Moreno y Daoiz requested his brother in Spain, Lieutenant General Tomás Moreno y Daoiz, to intervene directly with the Minister of War, Marqués de Campo Sagrado, to get him out of Mexico. Possession of this type of connection enabled some European officers either to flee the morass of an interminable conflict or to move out of army postings and into much more lucrative administrative jobs. Naturally, Spanish and Mexican creole officers lacking such ties resented this sort of manipulation that was not available to them.[21]

Particularly exasperating to ambitious Mexican officers was the ability of Europeans of the same or lower ranks and seniority to bypass them for the best military and administrative commands. Peninsular officers became provincial governors, intendants, and regional *comandantes* who exercised exceptional wartime powers. Through distribution of rebel properties, confiscations, and special taxation, many officers managed to accumulate fortunes for themselves and their subordinates. They were excessive in their expectations about the wealth of Mexican towns and districts to support expeditionary battalions and to accord financial subsidies to the royalist cause.

Colonel Melchor Alvarez, for example, arrived at Jalapa in 1813 with a *división expedicionaria* from Spain of 2,000 troops of the Regimientos de Infantería of Savoya and Extremadura. To avoid yellow fever, the force departed Veracruz quickly and arrived in the uplands at Jalapa with cash reserves sufficient for only 12 to 15 days maintenance.[22] Jalapa was a town of only 11,000 people with about 40 houses suitable for army billets. The ayuntamiento begged Viceroy Francisco Javier Venegas to alleviate excessive demands by Alvarez's division upon local resources. The town was in deep economic recession caused by the war that dramatically reduced urban income from commerce and agriculture. Notwithstanding declining fiscal expectations, over the past three years since 1810 the community had paid out 200,000 pesos to defray expenses of the expeditionary Regimientos de Infantería of Asturias, Lobera, Castilla, Zamora, and Fernando VII. In the case of the latter regiment, yellow fever contracted at Veracruz during a rebel-enforced blockade not only ruined military effectiveness, but cast an enormous burden of sick and convalescing soldiers upon the limited hospital facilities of Jalapa.[23]

Alvarez's imperiousness and his natural concern for the welfare of his soldiers caused him to dismiss entirely the financial woes of the Jalapeños. After an acrimonious exchange of notes, Alvarez asked Viceroy Calleja to dismiss the head of the ayuntamiento and to replace him with a "true Spaniard." In the colonel's view, the town leaders thought only of their own comfort and they were able to dominate local opinion. To terminate chronic feuding between civil and military leaders, Alvarez proposed that the viceroy appoint a governor of Jalapa who would unite the martial and civilian jurisdictions.[24] Calleja concurred, selecting Brigadier Joaquín Castillo y Bustamante to hold political and military command. The solution improved efficiency, but further eroded the powers of the traditional municipal governors and the local creole elite. Alvarez went on to become Comandante de Oaxaca, where he was caught red-handed in corrupt practices that exacerbated civil-military relations—fraudulent sales of insurgent property, misappropriation of tax funds, and authoritarian acts toward civilian officials and the populace. Viceroy Juan Ruíz de Apodaca recalled him to Mexico City for punishment, but later returned him to active duty. Alvarez served in the Sierra Gorda region where he became involved in fresh controversies. In 1821, he joined the rebellion of Agustín Iturbide.[25]

The predatory search for wealth and rewards by peninsular officers did nothing to advance the royalist cause among Mexicans. Over the decade of rebellion, creole officers felt growing resentment against Spanish commanders who were recent arrivals in the country. Lacking connections to the metropolitan appointments and patronage system, creole officers could do little to seek redress. Active campaigning and severed communications caused by the war made it difficult for officers to voice grievances through normal channels. Some stationed at major cities did file official complaints that were a warning of future conflicts. In one case, Colonel José María Echeagaray, a Veracruz born creole, labored for years in an unsuccessful effort to gain equal opportunity with successive peninsular officers who landed at Veracruz and received automatic preference for the better posts. If this was not bad enough, the negative attitudes of the newcomers galled their creole colleagues. Echeagaray noted, "it is a common rumor among recent arrivals from the peninsula that anyone born in the country (Mexico) is an insurgent."[26] He pointed out that the *hijos del país* who made up the majority of the army had played the essential role in combat against the rebel masses. In four major engagements and innumerable smaller battles, the creole army had turned back the tide of independence.[27]

Like their officers, European NCOs and soldiers were something of a two-edged sword for the royalist cause. To achieve victory, their professional skills were absolutely essential. On the negative side, their wanton disregard for the Mexican populace created more confirmed enemies than grateful friends. European soldiers carried the same haughty social and racial superiority of their commanders. They raised havoc with civilians and showed very little regard for the public good. Even in Mexico City, expeditionary soldiers robbed residents of their purses or coins. During 1815, even at midday, public squares and streets were not safe; some incidents occurred even within the sight of the city *regidores*.

The lower classes and especially the Indians who transported fruit and other provisions by canoe and burro for the markets were regular targets. If they refused to accept confiscation of their goods at the guardposts or to pay protection money, soldiers gave them terrible beatings. Sometimes the violence was totally gratuitous. On Sunday, October 17, 1815, troops from a European regiment seriously wounded a man with two bayonet thrusts and beat his wife when the couple could not produce a light for their cigarettes. Men of the Regimiento de Infantería of Zamora smashed shutters and doors, assaulted workmen, and seemed to take sport in robbing and molesting civilians. The attacks against persons and property became even more violent when rivalries between soldiers of different regiments spilled out of the taverns onto the streets.[28]

Some Mexican units of the royalist army were guilty of equally atrocious behavior and predatory attitudes. Soldiers of the Regimiento Provincial de Dragones Fieles de Potosí, a militia unit raised at the beginning of the Hidalgo Revolt, robbed and sometimes murdered civilians with near total impunity. Garrisoned at Izucar during 1820, several companies of the regiment attracted the denunciations of the ayuntamiento and many prominent residents who testified under oath about assaults, machete slashings, and NCOs who forced their way into fandangos with drawn sabers.[29] Much of the trouble in this regiment, as in many others, stemmed from the exhaustion of the long conflict. By 1820, men of the San Luis Potosí dragoons had been in active duty for ten years without a break. Recruited or simply removed from their families and given very little formal military instruction, they had been marched off to serve in small garrisons and detachments throughout Mexico. In 1818, their acting commander, Colonel Matías de Aguirre, informed Viceroy Apodaca that he could not submit accurate monthly reports on the status of the scattered companies. When he requested manpower lists and other information, either he received no response or a badly drafted document that was next to useless. Aguirre described his officers as unschooled in administration and accustomed only to chasing guerrilla bands.[30]

In 1819, some of the San Luis Potosí dragoons served on the *camino militar* between Jalapa and Veracruz, where they employed terror in search and destroy missions into the populated barrancas and isolated valleys. In a campaign designed to crush resistance in Veracruz province, they implemented orders to obliterate houses and buildings found outside protected zones, burn all crops and fruit trees, kill all livestock, and arrest any persons discovered without valid passports.[31] To gain victories and maintain the initiative, the royalist forces had to accept incredible hardships and sustain constant pressure so that the will of the insurgents cracked before their own. In the process, regular soldiers and militiamen became hardened to brutality through the years of counterinsurgency warfare. Many lost their humanity and the capability to identify friend from enemy.

In some royalist units, incidents of group violence by companies replaced individual acts committed by soldiers. In October 1820, soldiers of the Regimiento de Dragones de España stationed at the small town of San Martín in the province of Puebla became totally insubordinate and turned the whole community into anarchy. Brigadier Ciriaco de Llano, Military and Political Governor of Puebla, discovered that he lacked many options on how to solve deep rifts in the unit. He placed no trust in the colonel, lieutenant colonel, or the major of the Dragones de España—the latter officer was in charge at San Martín. While Llano recognized the necessity of removing these troops from San Martín, he did not want to have them in the Puebla garrison, which was full of amnestied former insurgents who he felt had not the best intentions. Since he believed that the dragoon officers held the same rebellious ideas of the soldiers, he was almost at a loss at how to redeploy the companies.[32] The solution decided upon by the army command could not have been more damaging to the royalist cause if it had been planned by the insurgents themselves! The first of two insubordinate companies was sent under Alférez Santiago Rodríguez to reinforce Colonel Iturbide, who had just taken command of operations in the rumbo de Acapulco.[33] They arrived just in time to join Iturbide's conspiracies and the Plan de Iguala.

Although the symptoms of exhaustion and insubordination were evident in the royalist army as early as 1818, the regime failed to acknowledge what was a terminal condition. Even among the elite expeditionary units, officers and troops tended to prevaricate rather than to face reality. They could not stamp out the centers or *focos* of insurgent power. Colonel Juan Rafols, ambitious commander of five companies of the Regimiento de Infantería de Murcia attached to the army of the Provincia del Sur, complained bitterly that Comandante General Brigadier Gabriel Armijo evaded opportunities to finish off the rebel chief Vicente Guerrero. Following the siege of Barrabas in January 1819, Guerrero retreated without provisions, supplies, or ammunition. Instead of engaging in an active pursuit, Armijo delayed. Finally he sent Rafols on a disastrous march through extremely inhospitable mountainous terrain that broke the morale of his troops and cost him most of his precious pack mules.[34] Rafols damned Armijo for covering up the unpalatable truth of his failures in order to paint a rosy picture of royalist successes against Guerrero and the even more sanguinary rebel chief, El Indio Pedro Asencio.

Rather than winning victories in the skirmishes in the mountainous country, the royalists were losing ground and being confined to their strongholds. Rafols's soldiers were dressed in rotting rags and often marched without shoes. In some areas, soldiers needed as many as four pairs of shoes per month. The Murcia infantrymen received none and their morale declined to such a level that many soldiers deserted due to a combination of misery and embarrassment of being naked. The meat given as provisions was rotten and the bread impossible for European Spaniards—corn tortillas rather than wheat bread and biscuit staples. If Rafols's situation was not bad enough, his men went for months without receiving their pay.[35]

Frustration, boredom, disgust with conditions, and other negatives compounded to influence both Spanish and Mexican officers. They saw themselves fighting a forgotten and grossly misrepresented war without adequate recognition or support. Their greatest grievance was lack of regular pay and allowances needed to provide for subsistence. While the army was able to extract sufficient funding until about 1818, economic conditions became worse rather than better until 1821. In August 1818, Lieutenant Colonel Juan Boixo of the expeditionary Regimiento de Infantería de Zaragoza garrisoned at Querétaro complained to Viceroy Apodaca that his unit was in desperate need of money. Of over 20,000 pesos owed for back pay, the Querétaro treasury offered only 6,223 pesos. The shortfall of 14,000 pesos left the soldiers with reduced provisions and worn-out uniforms and shoes. Some men circulated a *papel anónimo* blaming their senior commanders for their dire situation.[36]

Overcome by the suffering and criticism, the regimental commander, Brigadier Domingo Luaces, wrote to the viceroy that never in the history of the Zaragoza infantry — over 157 years — had the soldiers suffered so much and for so long. He traced his regiment's history through wars against France, Portugal, Britain, North African nations, and in Santo Domingo — concluding that the war in Mexico was by far the most destructive chapter. Lengthy campaigns, torrid heat, lack of food, and every sort of misery consumed regimental manpower, and the division of the unit into three separate sections made accurate accounting impossible. All account books and offices of the unit were in a state of total chaos. Like many other conventionally trained officers in New Spain caught in the mire of an endless guerrilla struggle, Luaces requested the assembly of his regiment in one location and time to rebuild depleted numbers.[37]

Viceroy Apodaca and his sub-inspector general, Brigadier Pascual Liñan, could not accept this criticism. The numerous garrisons and divisions at least held the rebels in partial check. Given the situation, it was impossible to assemble battalions, let alone entire regiments. The viceroy hoped that his policy of granting generous amnesties to exhausted insurgents would produce the victory that royalist arms had failed to win. He was correct in part with this approach, but he neglected to satisfy deep grievances emanating from his own army. He answered Luaces's assessment of his own regiment by the rather specious argument that the Zaragoza infantry which came to Mexico with Liñan in 1816 had received better treatment and postings than many other units.[38] This was not a useful exercise and Apodaca exacerbated existing complaints by personal attacks on Luaces rather than reforms to improve conditions and to arrange regular pay.

First, the viceroy attacked Luaces for feigning illness. Even though he doubted the reality of the medical condition, he granted the colonel two months leave in Mexico City. There, he noted Luaces's "robust good health" that confirmed his original suspicions.[39] Second, Apodaca chided Luaces for his inability to understand the nature of a guerrilla war in a country of such great size. In his view there was no other solution for the royalist army other than to divide regiments and battalions to create numerous small garrisons, divisions, and patrols. It was ridiculous even to suggest that a regiment should be employed against guerrilla bands that could not stand up to a company of regular troops. If the administration of the Regimiento de Zaragoza was in disorder and if the men were naked, insubordinate, and unpaid, Apodaca blamed Luaces, who he believed did not love his soldiers as much as his private affairs! On one occasion, the colonel had gone to Havana to attend to some private business.[40]

Clearly, Apodaca was out of touch with the reality of conditions in many of the regular and provincial militia units that made up his army. Many commanders expressed exactly the same grievances as Luaces, and the dilemma for the viceroy was that he had no solutions. In September 1818, he was willing only to admit that there had been some delays in paying units during active combat missions. He was angry at anonymous petitions and letters from the Regimiento de Zaragoza, which he took as a dangerous loss of discipline and good order. Judging from his own military career in Spain after 1808, Apodaca was certain that the troops must have suffered worse privations fighting against the French.[41] In fact, like his subordinate officers, the viceroy was caught in a war that consumed troops and resources without the prospect of definitive victory. Although Spain promised replacements, in reality the royalist army was allowed to erode, and with it went morale and essential civilian support.[42] Despite Apodaca's urgent appeals for 3,000 European soldiers in 1818, none were sent to fill the depleted companies of the expeditionary units. Instead, Mexican delinquents, criminals, and amnestied rebels accepted military service to evade prison or execution. The rot within the royalist army went unchecked, increasing the potential for disaster.[43]

Conditions in New Spain and in the Spanish empire as a whole seemed to conspire against the Mexican royalist army. In New Spain, 1820 was a disastrous year for the royalists that set the stage for the independence movement of Iturbide. First, notwithstanding Venadito's (Apodaca) official optimism, the guerrilla war ground on without end. Some insurgents were driven to accept pardons and found their units adopted intact into the royalist forces. In the guerrilla foco of the Provincia del Sur, the band of Padre Manuel Izquierdo became for a short while a royalist force under the command of Iturbide. In many respects, the amnesty program moved the enemy from without and placed it within the royalist camps, where it could help subvert loyal garrisons and make Iturbide's task much simpler.

Secondly, 1820 produced a climate-related setback in the crucial Bajío provinces that slowed the economic recovery and damaged the general morale of the population and of the royalist garrisons. Heavy rains in the Celaya and Irapuato region caused severe flooding of properties and mines. In the city of Irapuato alone, the waters inundated more than 1,000 houses.[44] Weather-related losses in mining, agriculture, and industry paralyzed the economy. The Comandante General of Guanajuato, Antonio Linares, reported a decline in mining output of fifty percent that reduced the income of the Real Hacienda. The *Alcabala* produced less revenue, tobacco monopoly income was reduced, and consequently, the provincial regime lacked sufficient money to pay the army garrisons. By August 1820, Linares was 15,000 pesos short of making up his military budgets to pay and maintain the units under his command, and his deficits were mounting.[45]

If the natural calamities did not have impact enough upon the royalist military, the renewal of the Spanish Constitution produced administrative chaos. The Constitution did not have a long enough run in Mexico to create new problems, but it exposed festering sores developed through the long years of rebellion. The strongest loyalists of Fernando VII — the administrators, army officers, and Church leaders — came to adopt independence as a means to save the country and the system they knew. For the royalist army, one of the most significant issues had to do with the *contribuciones militares* — the militia support taxes paid to maintain the *urbanos* and *rurales* who guarded the home front throughout New Spain. Often collected by the most arbitrary and brutal methods, the taxes hung like a great weight about the necks of Mexican subjects of all classes and regions. Indians who lacked half a real or a real for the tax found themselves despoiled of "their miserable rags" and left in shameful nudity. Some men received such terrible threats and beatings from the collectors that they were driven into the arms of the insurgents or to the extreme of suicide.[46] The Constitution dissolved the local *juntas de arbitrios* that had administered the militia taxes, and the new constitutional ayuntamientos of cities, towns, and villages were almost unanimous in declining to continue any form of the taxes. With the sudden loss of essential funding, the local militia structure crumbled.

In the light of events of 1821, the whole question of the *contribuciones militares* takes on very great importance. It was as if someone had released pressures built up for years. From Puebla, Ciriaco de Llano informed Viceroy Venadito that all of the constitutional ayuntamientos had sent delegations to complain about the weight of militia taxation and to report "the state of misery and backwardness of the contributors who had to pay the levies." In the view of all municipal leaders, not only was it impossible to collect from rich and poor, but it would be dangerous to press the issue. Desperate to retain what he could of the *urbano* and *rural* militias, Llano proposed the continuation of some forces to carry the royal mail and to undertake escort duty. His ideas produced instant protests and a new round of representations from the towns opposing even moderate militia taxation.[47] Municipal corporations that failed to protest simply let their companies disintegrate and disappear.

Since the ayuntamientos were totally responsible for the local militias—including enlistment, officer proposals, and everything to do with maintenance and internal administration—there was little Llano could do to halt the erosion. Except in the towns of Tlapa and Izucar, by the beginning of 1821 all of the *urbanos* and *rurales* of Puebla Province had been extinguished. Although a new Milicia Nacional was to have come into existence under the Constitution, nothing had been accomplished when the Iturbide Revolt swept through the province. Llano attempted to obtain control over surplus arms in the towns, but most of these went to support the new insurgent Army of the Three Guarantees. Embittered by the experience, Llano expressed not a little satisfaction when Iturbide's guerrillas raided towns that had disbanded their own defense forces.[48]

From the military as well as from various political perspectives, the Spanish Constitution was one more nail in the coffin of the royalists. Accustomed to ruling with an iron hand and without opposition, the old administrators resented any loosening of authority and criticism from the public. In some regions, the authorities lacked sufficient military control over towns of their jurisdiction to create constitutional ayuntamientos. They feared rebel raids brought on by efforts to elect municipal governments, and the people refused political activities in favor of the Spanish side that might cause them to lose their properties and even their lives.[49]

In other areas, the Constitution relaxed the discipline imposed by the harsh wartime regime. Loyal administrators reported an increase in drunkenness, quarrels, refusal to pay taxes, and other disorders.

The churches suffered declining attendance at Masses and schoolmasters complained that they were insulted by Indian pupils who refused to attend school. The administrator of Santa Ana, near Mexico City, informed Viceroy Venadito that the Spanish Constitution was "a printed patent that authorizes them [the Indians] to violate the law with impunity and to evade any recognized authority."[50] Many officials believed that the Indian and mestizo population lacked the sophistication to comprehend "even the most obvious principles of the new system." They possessed no knowledge of constitutional matters, did not speak the Spanish language, and depended totally upon their traditional system of working through their own old superiors.[51]

Similar complaints from all over central Mexico reveal the level of disintegration and chaos confronting the existing regime and the royalist army. Officers and civilian leaders found themselves radicalized by events that surged about them, threatening everything they had depended upon in their ordered lives. It is illustrative to trace individual careers through this period to assess the impact of events that would cast so many previously loyal civil servants and military personnel into acts of treason against their *patria*, and cause others to be dispossessed totally and exiled from the county they had adopted.

Beginning with Juan Rafols, whose loyalty to Spain never wavered, we can identify a growing stridency and negativism directed toward Mexico. Bogged down in a guerrilla war in the Provincia del Sur, Rafols sharpened his counterinsurgency techniques to a point of counterproductivity, and he turned upon the Indians, whom he could not comprehend. He described the rebel followers of Pedro Asencio as "*fieras*" [wild beasts] who "have no knowledge of God, religion, or of government." Rafols declared, "In my opinion these Indians are more idiotic now than they were prior to the conquest of this kingdom."[52] While he had attempted to grant provisional amnesties to Indians who would accept royal pardons, the guerrilla bands were able to recruit new fighters and to press their advantage whenever possible.

Some of the most active officers rejected the pacific programs of Venadito and sought their own solutions. In Veracruz province, young acting Captain Antonio López de Santa Ana followed his own ideas on how to deal with the insurgent enemy. Described by his superiors in 1819 as "active, zealous, and indefatigable," Santa Ana exceeded his orders as he led royalist militias against rebel bands operating just outside of the port city of Veracruz. When he apprehended an insurgent chief named Francisco de Asis, Santa Ana refused him the right to seek royal amnesty. Without taking time for even a summary trial, he ordered Asis executed by firing squad within sight of the walls of Veracruz.[53] This arbitrary act annoyed the Governor of Veracruz, who dismissed Santa Ana for taking matters into his own hands. The ambitious young officer went to the capital, where he informed Venadito that he deserved a reward and not punishment for his actions on behalf of the royalist cause.[54]

Beset by a confusing reform system and exhausted by the endless war, officers began to look for a savior to lead them. That man, Agustín de Iturbide, was himself pushed by a chain of events to the precipice that would lead him to declare for independence. Despite his established military career, legal complaints alleging misuse of funds were directed against Iturbide while he was Comandante General at Guanajuato and forced him to resign his post. For years he was left in a legal limbo and he grew increasingly angry at the viceroy who would not convoke a courtmartial to clear the charges. Iturbide was bitter that he had been forced to make "the degrading metamorphosis from warrior to litigant." More important, he realized that no matter what the outcome of his legal difficulties, there was bound to be grievous damage to his reputation and to his future military career.[55] Unable to obtain the kind of justice he wanted from the Spanish regime, Iturbide found that chance gave him an opportunity to circumvent existing structures. That chance was the appointment to replace the infirm Colonel Gabriel Armijo as Comandante General of the Provincia del Sur.

The fall of New Spain was remarkable for its brevity, considering the potential of existing military forces, and for its moderate effusion of blood. The Plan de Iguala of Iturbide attracted many different sectors of the Mexican population and was viewed as something of a panacea. If this was not true in reality, a great number of people, including soldiers, embraced at least some of its concepts. Almost immediately, the royalists lost whatever moral high ground remained to them, and there was no solid nucleus about which the loyalists could organize. Many detachment and garrison commanders, still good Spaniards, found that they were helpless witnesses to a celebration of independence that made them redundant. Their efforts to command fell upon deaf ears as soldiers and civilians joined to welcome the new Mexican nation months before the final victory.

At Altotongo, for example, Colonel Juan de Ateaga was a spectator to peaceful independence in March 1821, as his districts and towns joined spontaneous, jubilant celebrations accompanied by peals of bells, fireworks, and salutes by troops now loyal to the Mexican empire.[56]

At this juncture, Iturbide was not yet victorious, but the royalist cause was lost. Ateaga begged for a regular infantry company from Puebla "to cut out the cancer," not comprehending that many jurisdictions were in a similar state of collapse. Pardoned insurgents relapsed to recruit new bands that were welcomed as heroes and joined by regular army troops as well as civilians. Some royalist officers, such as José Joaquín Herrera, Anastasio Bustamante, and Luis Cortázar, jumped to join the revolt while others hesitated temporarily before making the definitive and irrevocable move to independence.[57]

Amidst the ruins of New Spain, even the most loyal officers were left in deep shock. Some attempted to continue operations or to launch unrealistic projects to restore royalist power. Viceroy Venadito compounded the disaster by concentrating his regular troops in Mexico City for a last stand—thus weakening outlying provinces that were not endangered immediately. From Valladolid [Morelia], Intendant Manuel Merino wrote that what he always had feared was now happening; Iturbide's rebels simply swept through his province recruiting the dispersed and isolated royalist garrisons. At the beginning of March 1821, he had a force in Valladolid of over 3,500 troops, but by April 4, the total had declined to only 1,500. Some 30 to 40 soldiers crossed over to the rebels daily.[58] At the city of Puebla, Brigadier Llano lost control to a people who believed independence to be victorious. The publication of Iturbide's plan in the periodical *La Abeja Poblano* on March 4 caused wild festivities, during which the crowd forced Llano to fire three cannonades and to call out the town musicians. As he explained later to the viceroy, to have resisted the populace would have caused a general riot.[59]

In the succeeding months, Llano faced a chain of shocks. On the night of April 12, an angry mob of 4,000 people gathered in front of the bishop's palace. Infuriated by a rumor that the regime had arrested the bishop, they yelled "¡Viva la independencia; muera el gobierno y los gachupines!" Gangs of civilians attempted to obtain firearms from the barracks of the Batallón Provincial de Comercio and many persons appeared with shotguns, pistols, swords, knives, and sharp instruments attached to poles. In the main plaza, a melee broke out between some members of the crowd and soldiers of the garrison. Someone opened fire and in the general confusion, the troops killed two civilians and wounded an additional eight. On this occasion, Llano managed to restore order, but it was clear that he had lost his capacity to govern.[60] Without fresh soldiers, he informed Venadito, the towns of Puebla province would declare for independence "en un minuto."[61]

Elsewhere, royalist commanders were equally impotent and swept up in a *fait accompli.* In the Bajío, Brigadier Antonio Linares fled from town to town, blaming his subordinates for giving up without a fight. He was stunned to see Guanajuato fall without a shot and enraged when Lieutenant Colonel Bartolomé Peño abandoned San Miguel to seek refuge at Querétaro.[62] Linares wanted a scapegoat, but he could not avoid filling the role personally. His defense of Celaya was a joke when all but a few companies in the garrison changed sides and embraced the insurgent cause. Linares, more or less free under loose guard, continued to write dispatches to the viceroy. He learned that he was held responsible for the collapse of his command.[63] Querétaro fell after a short skirmish and its commander, Brigadier Domingo Luaces, adopted the cause of independence. With a few of his men, Colonel Juan Rafols suffered terrible hardships as he retreated from Texupilco to Toluca and Mexico City. Rafols lost all of his possessions and he had to conduct his pregnant wife and young children on foot through the barrancas and mountain passes. These blows, combined with illness contracted in the campaigns of *tierra caliente,* prevented Rafols from playing an active role in the final collapse of Mexico.[64]

While the remaining senior commanders cowered in Mexico City, a few active officers, such as Colonel Francisco de Hevia and Colonel José Joaquín Márquez y Donallo, attempted to reverse the inevitable defeat. This time there was to be no escape. Hevia fell in combat at Orizaba and Márquez y Donallo led a quixotic expedition to open communications with Acapulco.[65] In the capital, Venadito and Liñán were hardpressed to construct defenses for the final struggle and to find senior officers who would command the rapidly eroding garrison. As the officers either changed sides or manufactured reasons why they could not accept active commands, their units were thrown into confusion.

On April 28, 1821, Captain Agustín de Elzora of the Dragones Fieles de Potosí explained to Sub-inspector General Liñán that the process of elimination made him senior officer remaining in his unit. Most recently, Major Joaquín Parres and the captain of greatest seniority, Miguel Barragán, had gone over to Iturbide, leaving the remaining officers "ashamed and discouraged." The few soldiers were naked and required powerful incentives in the form of arms, uniforms, equipment, horses, and most of all pay if they were to be reanimated.[66] A few days previously, Colonel Hevia reported that 32 Dragones de Potosí and 60 Dragones of the Regimiento del Príncipe deserted and were attempting to make their way home to Querétaro and the Bajío cities.[67]

The coup that overthrew Venadito and placed the sub-inspector general of artillery, Brigadier Francisco de Novella, on the viceregal throne did little to delay the final capitulation.[68] There was no royalist army of operations to crush the new insurgents. Iturbide and his subordinate commanders—many of whom were newly minted patriots—isolated and suppressed the remaining garrisons. By June 1821, just prior to his own overthrow and besieged by the flood of rebellion, Apodaca was reduced to smuggling concealed messages out of Mexico on scraps of paper. Desperate, he warned the imperial regime that Spain was on the verge of losing Mexico unless 8,000 to 10,000 troops arrived to rejuvenate the royalist army.[69] But the Spain of 1821 could not send a soldier to shore up the tattered centerpiece of its American empire. In a frank assessment of the capabilities of the metropolitan Spanish army dated September 1821, the *Consejo de Guerra* meeting in Madrid recognized that the military was in a state of general indiscipline and would not follow orders.[70]

Despite the situation, many prominent peninsular commanders shocked their comrades and families in Spain when they joined Iturbide's rebellion rather than staying with the old patria until the end. Some officers had been in Mexico for so long that they developed extensive financial interests and connections. Others disliked the antimilitary implications for Spain of the restored 1812 Constitution.[71] They anticipated greater advantages for themselves if they accepted Iturbide's promises to earn accelerated promotions and to maintain lucrative regional military commands. Brigadier Luaces advanced under the Mexican empire and in 1822 he confronted the remaining Spanish garrison at San Juan de Ulúa.[72]

The expectation of union between Europeans and creoles in the Plan de Iguala and the apparent dedication to monarchy proved to be irresistible lures.[73] The remaining Spanish loyalists found themselves without support or a capability to prolong the struggle. At the beginning of 1822, Brigadier Ciriaco de Llano found himself in Havana broken in health and destitute, but ready to give what aid he could to a reconquest of New Spain.[74] Although the future of the gachupín minority in Mexico was equally bleak, few of Iturbide's converts recognized the specter of anti-Spanish legislation and future expulsion laws under the Mexican republic. By the end of 1821, most royalists had become overnight patriots and few acknowledged any remaining ties to Spain.

/ 3

Los liberales y la Iglesia

Patricia Galeana de Valadés

El conflicto entre el liberalismo y la Iglesia católica sigue siendo uno de los temas capitales de la historia política de México, entre otras razones por su repercusión en la conformación de su Estado nacional. La vieja pugna entre el poder civil y el poder eclesiástico es motivo de análisis y de polémica hasta nuestros días.

La participación de la Iglesia en la vida de México fue determinante desde sus orígenes coloniales, lo que hace indispensable el conocimiento de la institución eclesiástica por todo aquel que pretenda comprender la historia de mi país y la mentalidad de su pueblo.

Como la historia de las ideas políticas[1] no se satisface en marcos teóricos economicistas ni de la microhistoria, sino que requiere de la perspectiva global del proceso histórico, en esta intervención intentamos dar una breve visión del conflicto entre los liberales y la Iglesia, presentando el proceso en su conjunto, para poder medir la transcendencia de acontecimientos que son causa de otros y no "meros antecedentes en el tiempo".[2]

Las creencias religiosas de los pueblos ocupan un lugar fundamental en su evolución social. En el caso particular de México la concepción católica del mundo se proyectó sobre el sistema social, político y económico y no a la inversa. De ahí que no sea posible estudiar la historia mexicana del siglo XIX sin comprender cabalmente su particular catolicismo, influido por la mentalidad indígena, eminentemente mágica y profundamente mística.

La lucha entre el cambio y la permanencia, entre el progreso y la ortodoxia, entre la modernidad y la tradición que se da en las sociedades de todos los tiempos, en el México del siglo XIX tuvo como protagonistas a la Iglesia por un lado y a los liberales por el otro. Es importante por lo mismo determinar hasta qué punto las concepciones religiosas que la mayoría de los liberales tenían, pudieron hacerse compatibles con sus proyectos de modernización social y política, así como el tradicionalismo religioso de los conservadores nonacentistas no fue obstáculo para que alentaran propósitos de avance económico e inclusive social, según se ve en el trabajo de la Maestra María del Refugio González.

El hecho contundente de que la occidentalización de México tuviera lugar a través de la religión católica, hizo a ésta constitutiva del ser nacional. Por ello, fue tan difícil la implantación de ideas que la Iglesia consideró heterodoxas. Por eso el punto de conflicto entre liberales y conservadores fue esencialmente la Iglesia, herencia de la cultura hispánica.

La secular institución eclesiástica se arraigó en nuestro territorio con la conquista, material y espiritual, de sus habitantes. Al independizarse México, la Iglesia reafirmó su dominio político en el país y constituyó un obstáculo para la consolidación del Estado nacional y de su sociedad civil, en la medida en que pretendió sujetar a ambos — Estado y sociedad — a los dictámenes de su corporación.

La Iglesia fue la institución política más poderosa y mejor organizada al inicio de la vida independiente de México. Era una "institución política" porque intervenía como protagonista en la organización del poder, porque sus miembros tenían ambiciones temporales que normalmente satisfacían aparejadas al ejercicio de su ministerio religioso; porque mantenían una férrea jerarquización de sus decisiones; y porque a lo largo de tres siglos de dominación se produjo una simbiosis entre las responsabilidades del gobierno de los hombres y el dominio de las conciencias.

Los eclesiásticos fueron autoridades civiles y ocuparon en la Nueva España cargos de primer nivel, llegaron inclusive a ser virreyes. De esta manera el clericalismo, condenado por la propia doctrina de la Iglesia,[3] quedó arraigado en los usos y costumbres del clero así como en la actividad pública. De ahí la dificultad para pasar de un Estado estamental a un Estado moderno, nacional y laico.[4]

La independencia política respecto de España constituyó también la independencia de la Iglesia católica mexicana del Regio Patronato que habían ejercido los reyes españoles desde la conquista de estas tierras, como una concesión del papado para facilitar la evangelización de sus naturales.

Con motivo del ejercicio del Regio Patronato, los monarcas españoles no sólo cobraban los diezmos para compensar los gastos de evangelización sino que nombraban obispos e intervenían en todos los asuntos internos de la Iglesia, al punto que la potestad civil llegó a interponerse entre la Iglesia y el Pontificado.[5]

Las facultades omnímodas del Regio Patronato fueron menores cuando se encontró en el trono un monarca débil. Todo esto dio por resultado una mezcla de asuntos políticos y religiosos comunes durante los trescientos años del virreinato. Esta fue una de las causas por las cuales posteriormente resultó tan difícil separar los asuntos de la Iglesia y del Estado en el siglo XIX.

Al independizarse México de España, la Iglesia se opuso a reconocer que el gobierno mexicano fuera heredero del Regio Patronato, al cual consideraba una concesión y no un derecho. La junta de diocesanos en 1822 sostuvo que con la Independencia cesaba simultáneamente el Patronato y que la Iglesia era autónoma y sólo obedecería a la curia romana.

De 1821 a 1855 los gobiernos mexicanos intentaron obtener el Patronato. Todas las constituciones del país lo mencionan entre las facultades del Congreso. La Constitución de 1824, por ejemplo, dice en la fracción XII del artículo 50 que el Congreso debe arreglar el ejercicio del Patronato en toda la Federación. La justificación era clara: México asumía plenamente su soberanía, y ésta era incompatible con la existencia de un poder compartido o con la tolerancia para que autoridades ajenas al país mantuvieran—u obtuvieran—facultades cuyo ejercicio dentro del territorio nacional hacía nugatorio el concepto de soberanía. El pontificado no otorgó el concordato a México, ni siquiera durante el segundo Imperio cuando estuvo en el trono un príncipe católico. Roma mantuvo una política displicente hacia México, que quedó incluso sin obispos en las primeras décadas de vida independiente.

Libre del Patronato y habiendo alimentado de caudillos al movimiento insurgente lo mismo que al bando contrarrevolucionario que, en aparente paradoja, llevó a la consumación de la Independencia, la fuerza política de la corporación eclesiástica se vio agigantada. Así el Estado independiente mexicano pasó a convertirse en una especie de Estado estamental, sin unidad del poder estatal, por estar éste compartido entre su depositario formal y quienes poseían la fuerza política y económica real. La institución eclesiástica tenía un gran poder económico derivado de sus dilatadas propiedades. Además de los militares, los verdaderos poseedores del poder eran los dueños de la tierra, en su mayoría en manos de la Iglesia.

Se ha calculado que la Iglesia poseía las tres cuartas partes de las tierras de cultivo.[6] Las raíces de su riqueza se remontan a la colonia cuando "la piedad o gratitud de unos, los remordimientos o el arrepentimiento de otros" fueron acumulando en manos de la corporación eclesiástica una buena parte de la riqueza del país.[7] Si bien es difícil cuantificar los bienes del clero, debido a que la corporación gozaba de fuero y sus propiedades escapaban al control del gobierno, puede asegurarse que constituía un "estado" rico dentro de un estado pobre. El arco del poder iba del dominio sobre los bienes al imperio sobre las conciencias. La corporación eclesiástica poseía el control de las voluntades por medio de la religión y a través del monopolio de la educación. El catolicismo tenía garantizada su preeminencia a través de la intolerancia religiosa, la censura en la prensa, los fueros eclesiásticos, la coacción civil para el cobro de las obvenciones parroquiales y el cumplimiento de los votos monásticos. Todo ello resultado de la integración de lo político con lo religioso.

Si en 1821 México logró consumar su independencia política de España, la independencia del Estado mexicano respecto de la Iglesia estaba aún lejos de lograrse. Después de conseguir la primera en una sangrienta guerra de once años, hubo que luchar por la segunda durante casi medio siglo de inestabilidad política y bancarrota económica. Los liberales dieron esta larga batalla.

Recordemos que en la edad moderna las ideas liberales se originaron en la reforma protestante, precisamente contra el catolicismo, el cual, no obstante haber surgido como una religión revolucionaria, al correr de los siglos había sido convertida por la jerarquía eclesiástica en un medio más de dominación, llevando a la pasividad de sus miembros.

La ideología liberal, como toda corriente de pensamiento, sufrió cambios a través del tiempo y de los espacios transitados, pero en México hasta 1873 fue esencialmente sinónimo de cambio. Téngase en cuenta que el encuadramiento esquemático de "liberales" y "conservadores" es en buena parte una manera convencional de aludir a individuos y grupos que presentaron en su época—y ofrecen desde la perspectiva de la nuestra—ciertas características de homogeneidad. No hubo, sin embargo, escuelas o partidos en el sentido europeo que nos permitan hablar de liberales o de conservadores como si entre unos u otros hubiera plena coincidencia de procedimientos y de objetivos.

Como sabemos, el liberalismo tuvo también manifestaciones diversas. El inglés fue más pragmático y el francés más teorizante, mientras que el primero se orientó a la economía, el segundo se preocupó más por la política.[8] El liberalismo inglés se desarrolló aquí, en los Estados Unidos, y ante el magnífico avance económico y político que este país logró en un corto plazo, se constituyó en el ejemplo que los liberales mexicanos trataron de imitar. Hubo también algunos mexicanos que leyeron a los ilustrados en su lengua original, aunque el liberalismo francés llegó a México principalmente a través de traducciones españolas, previamente expurgadas de ataques a la religión.

Si bien la mentalidad española se hizo extremista al calor de su lucha contra los moros, y fue España la cuna de la Contrarreforma, de las ideas teresianas y de los reyes católicos por excelencia, también ahí surgió un movimiento reformista en la segunda mitad del siglo XVIII, encaminado al sometimiento del clero. Carlos III, en su intento por modernizar al Estado español, dio medidas drásticas contra la corporación eclesiástica, como la expulsión de la compañía de Jesús, entre otras cosas por considerar que el cuarto voto de defensa del Papa implicaba un desafío para la soberanía del Estado. Posteriormente se logró más el control formal que el real; se sometió a la Iglesia mas no al clero.[9] El proceso reformista iniciado por Carlos III culminaría en México hasta 1867, con el triunfo de la Reforma republicana.

Después de los intentos reformistas de los borbones, el liberalismo tuvo en el México del siglo XIX seis diferentes etapas: el movimiento de Independencia, el primer intento reformista de 1833-34, la reforma de 1855-59, la legislación reformista del Segundo Imperio de 1864-65, la constitucionalización de las leyes de Reforma en 1873 y el liberalismo conservador del periodo dictatorial.

La primera etapa tuvo lugar a través del movimiento burgués ilustrado, con Miguel Hidalgo a la cabeza. El cura de Dolores, lector de los liberales franceses, personificó la lucha contra el absolutismo español y rompió con la ortodoxia eclesiástica, tanto por sus ideas heterodoxas en materia religiosa como por tomar las armas contra la corona española, aliada del pontificado.

El movimiento liberal insurgente de Hidalgo fue contrario al carácter laico de la revolución francesa. En su mensaje revolucionario Hidalgo introdujo el concepto de la defensa de la religión; pues conocía el profundo sentimiento religioso del pueblo mexicano, guadalupano.

Por su parte el movimiento popular de Morelos se encaminó en contra de las altas jerarquías eclesiásticas, enriquecidas por la corrupción; pero nunca atacó los principios de la religión. Podemos anticipar que, desde la raíz independentista, el liberalismo mexicano en el siglo XIX, excepto contadas excepciones, fue anticlerical y no antirreligioso.

Como la Independencia de México fue consumada por un movimiento contrarrevolucionario, la Iglesia conservó los privilegios de la época colonial. Las constituciones anteriores a la de 1857 consagraron la intolerancia religiosa y conservaron los privilegios de la Iglesia. A falta de unidad nacional, la religión fue el lazo de unión entre los mexicanos.

Desde el primer movimiento liberal de Independencia, la Iglesia se opuso al cambio: excomulgó a los insurgentes y convirtió las ideas de libertad en pecado; se negó a reconocer la independencia de México para defender el principio de autoridad representado por la corona española; y desconoció el principio de soberanía nacional, fundamento de los Estados modernos.

De 1821 a 1867 se desarrolló una lucha entre las ideas ilustradas nacionalistas, seculares, estatizadoras y progresistas y la ideología de la Iglesia católica, universalista, providencialista, corporativista, organicista y eterna.[10]

La vida política del México naciente se intentó organizar en logias masónicas, que fungieron como partidos políticos. La masonería fue reprobada por la Iglesia, las logias acabaron por perder fuerza. Mientras el Estado mexicano se debatía entre la monarquía y la república, entre el federalismo y el centralismo, la institución eclesiástica sólida, firme serviría de guía a la mayor parte de la población y de sus cuadros dirigentes.

El nada halagüeño panorama económico y la inestabilidad política de las primeras décadas de vida independiente llevó al primer movimiento de reforma en 1833. La generación de liberales que llevó a cabo este intento reformista, había vivido en su adolescencia el movimiento de Independencia y al ver frustradas sus esperanzas de prosperidad nacional, se convenció de la necesidad de acabar con las estructuras económicas, políticas y sociales que permanecían desde la Colonia. Se había logrado la independencia exterior al cortar el vínculo con la antigua metrópoli, pero subsistían las estructuras coloniales internas del país. Con objeto de fortalecer la autoridad del Estado combatieron los privilegios de las corporaciones y aumentaron las garantías de libertad individual para robustecer a la propiedad privada y crear una clase media de propietarios responsables.[11] El ideólogo de este movimiento, José María Luis Mora, pretendió robustecer al Estado con la asimilación de la Iglesia, para acabar con la existencia de un Estado dentro de otro.

En realidad, las convergencias eran mayores que las divergencias entre los liberales y conservadores en esta primera reforma.[12] Aun cuando tradicionalmente se habla de liberales y conservadores como grupos contrarios, en el aspecto económico tanto unos como otros coincidían en las ideas económicas del liberalismo, el respeto irrestricto por la propiedad privada y por las garantías individuales. Tan es así que la primera declaración de derechos aparece en las leyes conservadoras de 1836. La Iglesia es quien marca la división tajante entre ambos grupos al condenar a los liberales y a la legislación reformista.

El partido del progreso de 1833 pretendió resolver los problemas financieros del Estado con la desamortización de los bienes del clero. La Iglesia y sus partidarios armaron tal revuelo que Santa Anna, árbitro de la política nacional de aquella época, derogó la legislación reformista. Fracasó el primer intento de reforma, que resultó utópico frente al sentimiento popular. La minoritaria *élite* liberal apenas había logrado aplicar algunas medidas como la secularización de las misiones de las Californias y la clausura de la Universidad, estableciendo en su lugar centros de enseñanza pública en el Distrito Federal.

Esta primera tentativa fue todavía cautelosa; no llegó siquiera a establecer la libertad de cultos, que se consideró innecesaria dado que todo el pueblo era católico.[13] La idea central fue ejercer el Regio Patronato, designar autoridades eclesiásticas y transferir al Estado el sostenimiento del culto, aun sin la autorización del pontificado. El historiador católico Martín Quirarte se lamenta de que la Iglesia mexicana haya desaprovechado este aviso para autorreformarse y para mantener una posición menos vulnerable ante los embates del liberalismo. Es decir, no tomó conciencia de que los tiempos habían cambiado y de que la subsistencia de sus privilegios ya no era posible.[14] Por el contrario, la Iglesia se radicalizó en sus posiciones y llevó a la sociedad a una polarización total en el segundo movimiento de la Reforma.

La generación de liberales que llegó al poder al triunfo de la Revolución de Ayutla estaba constituida por un grupo más numeroso que el de '33, aunque todavía minoritario con relación a la mayoría del país, que era conservadora. Hubo diferencias entre la manera y el momento de aplicar la Reforma. El proceso de este tercer movimiento fue largo. Se inició con leyes reformistas en noviembre de 1855 y culminó con las Leyes de Veracruz en 1859-60.

El movimiento se radicalizó al surgir el enfrentamiento con la Iglesia. La primera de estas leyes, la de Juárez, fue un intento inicial para dar igualdad jurídica a los ciudadanos mexicanos, aunque subsistieron los tribunales eclesiásticos para asuntos de la propia Iglesia. Se dio libertad de prensa, cesó la coacción civil para el cumplimiento de los votos monásticos y el pago de obvenciones parroquiales y se suprimió a la Compañía de Jesús.

Con la pretensión de acabar con el poder económico y político de la Iglesia y de solucionar al mismo tiempo la bancarrota del erario, al igual que en 1833, se pensó en desamortizar los bienes de la Iglesia. Melchor Ocampo estuvo en desacuerdo con esta ley, llamada Lerdo, por considerar que reconocía tácitamente el derecho de propiedad de la Iglesia y por tanto legitimaba su defensa.[15] El ideólogo michoacano sostenía que la corporación eclesiástica tenía derecho de usufructo mas no de propiedad, ya que sus bienes eran de la nación.

Inmediatamente surgió la contrarrevolución encabezada por la Iglesia, al grito de "Religión y Fueros". Hubo manifiestos incendiarios como el de Tolimán, en Sierra Gorda (Estado de Querétaro), y rebeliones armadas, como la que encabezó el cura Francisco Ortega con los indios zacapoaxtlas de Puebla.

En este ambiente sesionó el Congreso Constituyente de 1856-57. La mayoría de los diputados eran moderados; pero la minoría liberal pura fue muy activa. Esta logró que en la Constitución quedara implícita la tolerancia de cultos. No obstante haber perdido la votación para decretar la libertad religiosa, además, se facultó a los poderes federales para que legislaran en materia de cultos. Asimismo, la Constitución incorporó las leyes reformistas de 1855 y 1856 así garantizando la libertad de enseñanza y de prensa; quitó el derecho de propiedad a las corporaciones religiosas; y suprimió sus fueros.

La Iglesia condenó a la Constitución por considerarla contraria a sus dogmas y enarboló su arma más poderosa: la excomunión. Además, promovió abiertamente una guerra de defensa de la religión. El resultado fue la guerra civil más sangrienta que sufrió el país después de la Independencia. La sociedad se polarizó a un punto tal que ambos grupos prefirieron recurrir al auxilio extranjero antes de permitir el triunfo de sus opositores.

Al calor de la guerra se dictaron la Leyes de Reforma. La Iglesia imprimió a la contienda un carácter de guerra de religión. Satanizó a la reforma, presentándola ante el pueblo como un ataque a sus creencias.

Las leyes de Veracruz tuvieron una gran diferencia con las de 1833. Ahora no se trataba de absorber a la institución eclesiástica y convertirla en un órgano del Estado, sino de separar definitivamente a la Iglesia del Estado; nacionalizar sus bienes; quitarle sus fueros, como el monopolio educativo, el registro civil; y suprimir las corporaciones religiosas y el pago de obvenciones parroquiales. Por todo ello, al triunfo de los liberales en la guerra, la Iglesia apoyó a la intervención francesa, como un mal necesario, para "evitar un mal mayor" y salvar así a la religión.[16]

Con todo, es preciso subrayar que no existió persecución religiosa. Lo que se combatió fue el clericalismo, contrario a la propia doctrina de la Iglesia. Los liberales mexicanos eran en su mayoría creyentes;

existe un sinnúmero de pruebas de la religiosidad de Juárez, cabeza del gobierno liberal.[17] La misma Constitución de 1857 había sido jurado en nombre de Dios. Las leyes de 1859 fueron decretadas bajo la presión de la guerra. Esto no quiere decir que los liberales carecían de convicciones, en cuanto a que era indispensable someter a la corporación eclesiástica para crear un Estado Nacional y organizar una sociedad civil; pero nunca pensaron perseguir a la religión que ellos mismos profesaban. Fue una lucha política, no una guerra de religión.

El Segundo Imperio, establecido por la intervención francesa con el apoyo de la Iglesia, constituyó un nuevo impacto del liberalismo europeo en México, que vino a dar la razón a reforma juarista.

La Iglesia mexicana y sus partidarios se pusieron en manos de Napoleón III, quien deseaba guardar ante el mundo una fachada de liberal, en oposición a las corrientes conservadoras de Prusia y Austria.[18]

A diferencia de su hermano, Maximiliano de Habsburgo era liberal. Ratificó las leyes dictadas por la reforma mexicana, mezclando principios de 1833 y 1859. Sancionó la nacionalización de los bienes del clero, decretó la libertad de cultos y, como príncipe católico, pretendió ejercer el Regio Patronato. Llevó a cabo una tercera reforma, desde la perspectiva de un príncipe católico, consciente de la necesidad de estas reformas para fortalecer al Estado. Su política liberal fue afín a su patrocinador, Napoleón III, y a la que su antepasado, José II, había puesto en práctica en Austria en el siglo XVIII.

La Iglesia se vio atónita como el supuesto salvador de la religión, el príncipe católico Fernando Maximiliano de Habsburgo, puesto por Napoleón, no respondió a sus expectativas. Por ello, comenzó a hostilizarlo. El Papa le negó el concordato; no podía sentar un precedente así en lo que consideraba su bastión, América Latina, y menos ante un imperio tambaleante. Al ser abandonado por Napoleón III, Maximiliano claudicó de su política liberal y buscó desesperadamente el apoyo de la Iglesia.

El Imperio nunca tuvo posibilidades reales de éxito, pero debe admitirse que contribuyó a la consolidación de la reforma liberal y a la unificación del Estado nacional. La intervención militar más larga que ha sufrido México hizo que el pueblo identificara como un conjunto a las bayonetas francesas, a la idea de monarquía, a los jerarcas eclesiásticos y al imperialismo extranjero. Se logró así el establecimiento de una sociedad civil, base de la soberanía y elemento indispensable de un Estado nacional.

Por fin pudo ponerse en práctica el proyecto liberal de nación que implicaba la organización de un Estado soberano, civil y laico. El Estado liberal logró el establecimiento de una sociedad civil, al acabar con los privilegios de las corporaciones eclesiástica y militar, al darse la separación entre Iglesia y Estado y al decretarse la libertad de cultos. En materia económica coincidió con los conservadores en el respeto a la libertad de empresa y a la propiedad privada. Pero significó el fin de los bienes en manos de las corporaciones, afectando con ello no sólo a la Iglesia, sino también a las comunidades indígenas. Estableció la igualdad frente a la ley y, en el ámbito cultural, significó el fin del monopolio educativo en manos de la Iglesia.

Uno de los aspectos sobresalientes del liberalismo mexicano del siglo XIX es la exacerbación del individualismo. Las libertades de culto y de enseñanza, además de la idea de un Estado laico, tendían a robustecer el principio del individualismo, como elemento fundamental de la política liberal del siglo XIX. El liberalismo mexicano no constituyó una ideología atea o antirreligiosa, pero, por su carácter individualista, era opuesta al carácter absolutista de la religión católica. Por ello pretendió someter a la corporación eclesiástica a los derechos individuales y al interés nacional.

Fue hasta la quinta etapa del liberalismo en México, según el esquema propuesto, cuando se dio carácter constitucional a las Leyes de Reforma. Durante el gobierno de Sebastián Lerdo de Tejada, en 1873, pudo incorporarse la legislación liberal a la Constitución en un largo y difícil proceso que se inició desde noviembre de 1870. A partir de entonces "la sociedad mexicana es secular por mandato constitucional".[19]

Lerdo de Tejada representó el ala radical de los liberales. Al llegar a la presidencia aplicó con rigor la legislación reformista que Juárez, con visión de estadista, no había considerado necesario aplicar, en primer lugar porque ya se había vencido a la Iglesia como poder político y además por no querer herir el sentimiento religioso del pueblo. Hay que recordar que uno de los primeros actos del gobierno juarista después de obtener la victoria en 1867 fue lanzar un plebiscito mediante el cual, además de reformas importantes como la creación del Senado, pretendió devolver el voto pasivo a los miembros de la Iglesia. Es un acto que prueba la ecuanimidad del liberal oaxaqueño.

Mientras Juárez se mantuvo firme en las decisiones fundamentales, como la separación entre la Iglesia y el Estado, transigió en aspectos menores, como era la manifestación de culto externo. Lerdo, en cambio, no permitió manifestaciones públicas de culto; exclaustró a monjas de la Ciudad de México y expulsó a las Hermanas de la Caridad. Todas estas medidas extremas le acarrearon no sólo la censura de los conservadores, sino de los propios liberales también.

El triunfo del liberalismo inglés contra el absolutismo monárquico desde el siglo XVII, representó el inicio de lo que posteriormente serían los regímenes constitucionalistas como garantía de las libertades públicas. Por eso, el liberalismo fue el apoyo de las garantías democráticas en el siglo XIX. Pero las tendencias liberales, una vez que se instalaron en el poder y que entraron al proceso constitucionalista, adoptaron una política inmobilista que se ha llamado "conservadurismo liberal". En Francia, por ejemplo, a partir de la crisis de 1848, surgió el temor de que el orden establecido fuera vulnerado por la insurgencia social y transformó a los liberales en conservadores: conservadores del poder.[20] En México este proceso se inició durante el último gobierno de Juárez y culminó durante el porfirismo con un conservadurismo abierto que condujo al Estado a seguir una política tolerante con la Iglesia y a que ambas instituciones estrecharan relaciones.[21]

En México la derrota de la Iglesia, de los conservadores y de la Intervención francesa, hizo posible la unificación popular en torno al gobierno nacional. Los liberales dejaron de ser una minoría satánica al convertirse en defensores de la soberanía nacional. Pero una vez en el poder, los liberales se tornaron en conservadores de la paz y el orden y los conservadores, en tradicionalistas.

Tal situación sería uno de los tantos puntos criticados por los opositores de la dictadura porfirista. Los "clubes" políticos precursores de la Revolución social de 1910 se llamaron a sí mismos liberales. El Círculo Liberal Ponciano Arriaga se pronunció en contra de la beligerancia que la Iglesia y el clero habían alcanzado, a ciencia y paciencia del régimen porfirista. De esta manera, el liberalismo decimonónico fue rescatado por la Revolución y reconocido como su antecesor.

La vigencia del liberalismo en México puede apreciarse hasta nuestros días, cuando todavía parece que la polémica liberales-conservadores, Iglesia-Estado, no está liquidada y se siguen discutiendo las Leyes de Reforma y las relaciones con el Vaticano. Sin embargo, como diría Guillermo Prieto, las leyes liberales están enraizadas en la historia misma de México.

La independencia entre la Iglesia y el Estado es un divorcio indispensable para que la libertad religiosa sea verdadera y no utilice la religión como medio de manipulación de ni campaña política.

El estudio decimonónico nos lleva a la comprensión del México actual enmarcado todavía dentro del horizonte liberal. Muchas de las ideas rectoras del Estado mexicano, fundado por los liberales, siguen estando vigentes así sea con formas de expresión distintas a las de origen.

# 4

El pensamiento de los conservadores mexicanos

María del Refugio González

En las páginas siguientes presento algunas ideas para el estudio del pensamiento conservador mexicano decimonónico. Se trata sobre todo de hipótesis de trabajo. En este ensayo se presentan algunos de los primeros resultados de mi investigación sobre el tema, pero evidentemente los enunciados con los cuales pretendo delimitar o perfilar el pensamiento conservador, deben ser verificados en personajes representativos de las diversas generaciones que actuaron, sobre todo en la vida política, entre 1808 y 1867. Sólo de esta manera podrá saberse a ciencia cierta si estas hipótesis de trabajo no están equivocadas.

Conservar es hacer que una cosa dure, cuidar de su permanencia, mantenerla en buen estado procurando que no se deteriore, que subsista íntegra, o poco menos. Los sujetos que realizan esta acción serán conservadores. En el terreno de las ideas políticas, el pensamiento o el estado de ánimo que los lleva a realizarla, podría llamarse conservadurismo. Ahora bien, en ese campo, el de las ideas políticas, en todos los tiempos ha habido corrientes de pensamiento que buscan conservar algo que ya existe, que se considera socialmente valioso, y que se halla amenazado de extinción, de ahí que a través de diversos medios se busque su conservación. El conservadurismo moderno surgió como reacción en contra de los postulados de la Revolución francesa. A partir de entonces este vocablo adquiere una connotación específica que hace referencia precisamente a lo que la Revolución pretende modificar dentro del aparato social en que se produce. El vocablo así entendido comenzó a utilizarse en la propia Francia a partir de 1815 y paulatinamente se extendió su uso a otros países que habían recibido la influencia de las doctrinas igualitarias y libertarias que alcanzaron su máxima expresión en la "Declaración de los derechos del hombre y del ciudadano" en 1789.

El pensador que dio articulación al conservadurismo en la forma antes señalada fue Edmund Burke, quien en sus *Reflexiones sobre la Revolución de Francia*...[1] analizó las "funestas" repercusiones que la doctrina revolucionaria había de tener en la sociedad. El pensamiento conservador se manifestó en cada país en forma distinta. Sin embargo, es una corriente de pensamiento que tiene algunos postulados que permanecieron más o menos inmutables durante casi cien años. A algunos de ellos se ha de hacer referencia a lo largo de las siguientes páginas. Por ahora basta señalar que en su esencia el conservadurismo busca la permanencia de las instituciones y las prácticas que han ido evolucionando en una sociedad a lo largo de su desarrollo histórico, ya que esa forma de evolución es garantía de su arraigo en la sociedad y, en consecuencia, de sus bondades.

El pensamiento conservador sólo puede ser estudiado en contraste con el pensamiento que pretende destruir lo que aquél busca conservar y como en cada país el sistema a combatir tenía sus peculiaridades propias, también las tiene el intento conservador. El esquema ideal propuesto por Lefevre para entender la Revolución francesa, que en este caso sería prototípica, considera a ésta como una consecuencia de cuatro movimientos distintos: una revolución aristocrática, una revolución burguesa, una revolución campesina y una revolución de las clases trabajadoras urbanas. Esta diversidad explicaría por qué es precisamente en la Revolución francesa y a consecuencia de ella que confluye y se articula una gran cantidad de postulados doctrinarios que venían proponiendo, desde tiempo atrás, la libertad natural del hombre, la igualdad, la razón como instancia definidora de la acción humana —la cual no derivaría en adelante de los designios de la Providencia—, la negación del derecho divino de los reyes y la necesidad de legitimar el ejercicio del poder en un contrato entre el monarca y los gobernados.

Es claro que no todos los movimientos arriba señalados se dan en todos los países que recibieron la influencia de la Revolución francesa, pero también es claro que en todos ellos se produjo un deseo de conservar lo que las ideas revolucionarias pretendían destruir, esto es, un movimiento conservador que admite, por lo menos, el mismo número de variables que su contrario: el pensamiento liberal. Ambos a veces se tocan y otras veces se separan, y no hay ningún obstáculo doctrinario para que un conservador, en el sentido político, actúe como liberal en el económico y viceversa.

Sin embargo, a decir de los entendidos en filosofía política, el conservadurismo ha mantenido algunos enunciados no liberales acerca de la naturaleza humana que permiten no sólo su identificación, sino su confrontación con los postulados del liberalismo. Se ha dicho que consciente o inconscientemente, en forma literal o metafórica, los conservadores tienden a asumir en la política la doctrina cristiana que postula el pecado original, con todas sus consecuencias. Aquí, a decir de esta corriente de opinión, radica una clave para la diferenciación entre conservadores y liberales. Los primeros no creen—como Rousseau, Voltaire y otros filósofos—en la bondad natural del hombre. El conservadurismo así concebido sería más un estado mental que una ideología, aunque también pueda llegar a ser ésta. Este estado mental a menudo se encuentra vinculado o se deriva de la adscripción de estos sujetos a alguna forma establecida de religión. Tienden a ver la sociedad de acuerdo al esquema que esa religión ha trazado.[2]

Si bien en lo antes señalado podría radicar la esencia del pensamiento conservador,[3] es claro que, en sus manifestaciones prácticas, la forma en que ese pensamiento puede constituirse en un programa político de acción varía en cada lugar. En el caso de México, las variantes se derivan de las condiciones impuestas por la realidad social y política de lo que fue la Nueva España. Mi tarea, pues, será proponer en las páginas siguientes algunas ideas para la interpretación del pensamiento conservador mexicano antes de 1867.[4]

La primera cuestión que parece importante dilucidar para poder identificar la naturaleza del pensamiento conservador mexicano dentro del marco temporal, arriba señalado, estriba en averiguar qué pretenden sus seguidores conservar y cuál es el programa—si es que lo hubo—que se trazaron para lograr sus objetivos. Si el conservadurismo encuentra su justificación en que busca la permanencia de algo que ya existía y que a consecuencia de uno o varios hechos se ve amenazado, tenemos que ver qué es lo que existía y de ello qué pretenden conservar.

Antes de seguir adelante parece necesario advertir que no todos los conservadores mexicanos propusieron la vuelta al régimen de dependencia política con España. Es importante señalarlo porque la restauración del antiguo régimen en términos generales no postulaba la posibilidad de que México volviera a ser dependiente de España y los intentos monarquistas tampoco lo contemplaron. En general, las soluciones partían de la idea de que, fuera cual fuera la forma de gobierno—y evidentemente tenían preferencias—, no podría ser otra que la que la nación, en forma independiente, pudiera darse.[5] Este hecho, que les venía dado por la antigua condición colonial, descalificó de entrada la restauración en beneficio de un soberano legítimo que hiciera depender su poder, en última instancia, de su derecho divino. Era precisamente en contra de un soberano que consideraron no legítimo que se enderezó el movimiento de independencia, que no la insurrección de 1810.[6]

La insurrección de 1810, en sus orígenes monarquista, resquebrajaba el orden constituido a medida que iba avanzando y, aunque no abarcó todo el territorio mexicano, sus repercusiones se dejaron sentir en el corazón mismo del virreinato. La convulsión social que llevaba aparejada habría tenido que desembocar en la constitución de una nueva sociedad, de haber triunfado el movimiento insurgente. En el Acta Solemne de la declaración de la América Septentrional del 6 de noviembre de 1813 se establecía claramente que se recobraba "el ejercicio de su soberanía usurpado". La nueva sociedad, en el peor de los casos, habría de partir del contrato social. La independencia, por su parte, fue simplemente una decisión política y no tenía por qué conducir al establecimiento de una nueva y distinta sociedad. Los partidarios de la independencia, tanto en su vertiente liberal como en la conservadora, habían percibido las consecuencias de los levantamientos populares y esto los hace, de entrada, más conservadores en el aspecto social que lo que sus ideas económicas o políticas podrían hacernos pensar que eran.

Si aplicamos el esquema elaborado por Lefevre para el caso de la insurrección y la independencia tendríamos que en la primera podrían haber triunfado tres de los movimientos que confluyeron en la Revolución francesa: la revolución burguesa, la campesina y la de las clases trabajadoras urbanas. Pero no fue así; para 1815 la insurgencia había sido sofocada y a la independencia concurrieron exclusivamente los burgueses. Ahora bien, dentro de esa burguesía que consiguió finalmente la independencia, se plantearon diversas y encontradas opiniones en torno a una gran cantidad de cosas, y también muchas similitudes. Si analizamos qué es lo que unos querían conservar y lo que los otros querían modificar, quizá estemos en el camino de comenzar a comprender la naturaleza del conservadurismo mexicano.

La tarea de revisar cómo fue "la última Nueva España", ha sido realizada en forma muy aguda por Roberto Moreno. Sin embargo, por deformación profesional — me dedico a la historia del derecho — me gustaría completar el esquema que él ha trazado con algunos datos que nos proporciona la historia institucional pero que, a mi juicio, repercuten en la historia social y política, y de ahí en el pensamiento de unos y otros. Estos son, en consecuencia, elementos valiosos para analizar el comportamiento de las clases "ilustradas" a lo largo del periodo que aquí se revisa. Dado que mi interés se centra en las instituciones y el derecho, nunca me parecerá ocioso insistir en que la Nueva España estaba constituida formalmente por dos Repúblicas: la de los indios (mayoritaria) y la de los españoles (minoritaria). Dentro de esta partición ideal hubieron de hacerse campo los mestizos, los negros y las castas. A todo esto se le fueron dando soluciones jurídicas.[7]

Veo, pues, a la Nueva España constituida por una sociedad estamental en la que los estratos se hallaban diferenciados jurídicamente. En el seno de esa sociedad era posible la movilidad social, sobre todo por razones económicas. La presencia de esos grupos o estamentos sociales dio lugar a una falta casi total de integración de la población, salvo en los núcleos urbanos, a la cual se debe agregar la existencia de enormes contrastes en lo social y lo económico. La República de los indios estuvo en posibilidad de elegir autoridades locales, las cuales siempre se hallaron subordinadas a los gobernantes distritales o provinciales. Por su parte, la población española o a la española atravesó los 300 años de gobierno colonial sin la experiencia de la participación política, aunque fuera indirecta, ya que incluso los cargos concejiles que hubieran podido ser de elección acabaron por venderse o beneficiarse al mejor postor. Sobra decir que los gobiernos distritales y provinciales también se beneficiaron, aunque, siguiendo las directrices de la Corona, debía buscarse que concurrieran a las subastas sujetos idóneos para ocupar los cargos. La venta y el beneficio de los oficios produjeron un entramado de clientela política vinculado a los hombres que podían financiar la compra de dichos oficios, lo cual fue factor determinante en la formación de poderosas oligarquías locales, algunas de las cuales necesariamente se vincularon al capital mercantil o minero.

Esa sociedad de grandes contrastes era gobernada por un rey que, desde un punto de vista jurídico, tenía carácter absoluto, aunque por la escasez de vías de comunicación se dio, de hecho, una amplia descentralización en algunos aspectos del gobierno y la administración de justicia. La pirámide del ejercicio del poder no contemplaba la separación de funciones, de ahí que en todas las esferas de dicho ejercicio se diera el fenómeno de la acumulación de funciones. Este hecho no fue modificado por la Ordenanza de Intendentes de 1786. A más de la acumulación de funciones, la doctrina jurídica preconizaba una idea patrimonialista del Estado y del oficio público; la idea del servicio público propuesta por las reformas derivadas de la implantación de la Ordenanza de Intendentes no había arraigado en el ánimo de los vasallos novohispanos al tiempo de proclamar la independencia.

Ese gobernante, el rey, jurídicamente absoluto, sólo compartía el poder con la Iglesia, de cuya cabeza había recibido sus dominios. De manera que aunque se hallaban, también jurídicamente, diferenciados el poder temporal y el espiritual, había una gran convergencia entre ambos, y también muchas pugnas. Sin embargo, estas pugnas no llevaban la sangre al río, ya que la monarquía hispana era católica y sus fines se inspiraban en las doctrinas del catolicismo de aquella época. Así, aunque en virtud del regalismo se había ido formando una "iglesia nacional" más vinculada al rey que a la Santa Sede, en la práctica, Estado e Iglesia tenían los mismos fines. Esto no debe contemplarse como un dato más que contribuye a conformar el esquema, sino quizá, como el más importante. La Iglesia condenaba las doctrinas individualistas que conducían a la idea del pacto social. A más de la identidad de fines entre la Iglesia y el Estado, debe señalarse respecto de la primera que era detentadora de una riqueza considerable y, sobre todo, era la institución más estable.

En lo económico la Nueva España tenía también grandes contrastes. Podemos comenzar diciendo que su política fiscal fue diseñada siguiendo siempre las necesidades prácticas de la Corona y que, en consecuencia, los ramos de la Real Hacienda, de la cual se pagaban los gastos del aparato eclesiástico, obedecían muchas veces a las necesidades del momento más que a una planeación preestablecida. Por lo que toca al comercio a gran escala, ultramarino y local, se puede decir que se diseñó una política proteccionista de los productos metropolitanos y se pusieron todo género de trabas al comercio local. A esto debe agregarse el comercio forzado, esto es, el repartimiento de mercancías que se hallaba en manos de gobernantes distritales y provinciales. El abastecimiento de las ciudades y el comercio indígena saldrían del planteamiento general aplicable al comercio ultramarino y su consecuente red de distribución local. Por otra parte, el contrabando encontró tierra fértil para su desarrollo a todo lo largo y lo ancho del virreinato. Finalmente, debe señalarse la existencia de mercancías estancadas explotadas en todas sus fases, incluida la comercialización, por la propia Corona o arrendadas a particulares. A ellas se agregan los estancos especiales creados en el siglo XVIII.

En el terreno de la administración de justicia, la Nueva España era un mosaico de fueros y privilegios concedidos en atención a la actividad que cada quien desarrollaba en la sociedad, pero también por el origen de los vasallos. En el primer sentido se encontraban los tribunales eclesiásticos, los mercantiles, el de minería, los militares, los universitarios, y en el segundo, el Juzgado General de Naturales.

Por lo que se refiere al trabajo, el régimen contemplaba desde la esclavitud hasta la prestación libre de obra y servicios. Por importante que haya sido esta última, la mayoría de la población se hallaba al margen del régimen de prestación libre de obra y servicios.[8] Dentro de este mosaico social y económico, a decir de los conservadores, lo único que permitía una cierta identidad era la religión. En otros lugares la "identidad nacional" se basa en una cierta semejanza de cultura, lengua y costumbres. Aunque en ningún lugar hay— ni ha habido—una identidad total y completa entre los diversos miembros de la sociedad, es claro que en el caso de la Nueva España esa identidad era todavía más remota en virtud de estar constituida como una sociedad dual: moderna y arcaica, rica y pobre, dinámica y estática, ilustrada y ágrafa, católica a la manera española y convertida—no siempre en forma pacífica—al catolicismo, absolutista y democrática. En los ejemplos anteriores el factor utilizado en el segundo término corresponde a la República de los indios. Los de en medio eran pocos, por lo menos hacia 1821.

Dentro de este complejo aparato social, económico y político debían implantarse otros elementos: la igualdad; la libertad de prensa, circulación y credo; la división de poderes; la asistencia pública; el sufragio universal directo; la unidad de jurisdicción; y el comercio libre. Los conservadores, en el sentido aquí señalado, se opondrían a modificar todo aquello que tocaba los derechos de la Iglesia. Se incluyen entre éstos tanto los que le correspondían por derecho divino como los que el derecho humano le otorgaba. Esto es lo que había venido sucediendo durante 300 años, y no había por qué cambiarlo.

A partir de 1821 se buscó constituir al país que surgía a la vida independiente como monarquía, república central o república federal. Las condiciones sociales y económicas heredadas de la época colonial y los hábitos políticos de los mexicanos impondrían a liberales y conservadores la necesidad de adaptar su pensamiento, originalmente elaborado en los países europeos, a las posibilidades de acción reales que ofrecía su propia circunstancia.

Si tenemos en cuenta lo que hasta aquí se ha señalado estaríamos en el camino de explicarnos algunas cosas, pero también estaríamos frente a la necesidad de reducir a unos cuantos enunciados el meollo del pensamiento conservador de aquellos años. ¿Por qué digo esto? Para los estudiosos del siglo XIX mexicano son familiares las contradicciones que en algunos aspectos presentan tanto los liberales como los conservadores, si hemos de tomar como parámetro el credo difundido por la Revolución francesa y su respuesta en contrario.

Todos hemos visto que son precisamente dos textos tachados de conservadores los que primero consagran los derechos individuales del hombre. Primero, el Estatuto provisional del Imperio mexicano, en forma clara pero no articulada, y después, las Siete Leyes de 1836, ya en forma articulada. Esta garantía, por el carácter centralista de ambos textos, abarcaba todo el territorio nacional. Asimismo, hemos visto cómo gobiernos tachados de conservadores intentan poner en circulación bienes eclesiásticos, aunque en forma discreta, mucho antes de la promulgación de las Leyes de Reforma. También hemos leído en textos constitucionales conservadores o simplemente en textos jurídicos elaborados por pensadores conservadores, la reivindicación del patronato y la necesidad del *placet* del congreso para que se aplicara la legislación pontificia. Por último, hemos podido observar en alguna de las constituciones de signo monárquico plasmado el principio de la soberanía nacional, sólo admitido anteriormente en el seno de las Cortes de Cádiz o por los insurgentes. Por otra parte, a lo largo del periodo que me toca explicar, muchas veces los conservadores proponen medidas económicas que podrían ser suscritas por liberales. Y por el contrario, éstos le establecen restricciones, por ejemplo, a la representación, que gustosamente suscribieron los conservadores.

La pregunta que surge inmediatamente es ¿por qué todo esto? Quizá la respuesta esté en que, como se afirmó en el primer apartado de este ensayo, no existe inconveniente doctrinario para que un conservador en el terreno social se muestre liberal en el económico y viceversa. Si hemos de reducir la esencia del conservadurismo a unos cuantos enunciados, estaría de acuerdo con los que afirman que el conservadurismo es una asunción política de la doctrina cristiana que postula el pecado original, con todas sus consecuencias, y de ahí la necesidad de brindarle al hombre ciertas instituciones para su salvación.[9] La institución encargada de este cometido es, por supuesto, la Iglesia.

Por otra parte, Jorge Adame, quien ha estudiado el pensamiento social de los católicos mexicanos a partir de la República restaurada, afirma que los católicos de esa época no son conservadores, sino tradicionalistas, y pienso que tiene razón. Su afirmación se basa en que los católicos de la República y la Dictadura carecieron de un programa de acción política. Así pues, tendríamos los dos elementos que permitirían identificar los conservadores de la época anterior a la que estudia Adame: su adscripción a la doctrina cristiana, entendida en su forma tradicional, y un programa de acción política. Este último sólo está presente en México hasta 1867. La última esperanza que tenían los conservadores mexicanos para impedir la separación de la

Iglesia y el Estado, con todas sus consecuencias, había muerto en las Campanas, después de defraudarlos.

A partir de la Restauración de la República, la separación de la Iglesia y el Estado es un hecho consumado, cotidiano, impuesto por la realidad jurídica del país. De esta manera, conservadores en sentido estricto sólo hubo en México mientras se pudo luchar por conseguir que se mantuvieran intocados los dogmas de la doctrina cristiana y las atribuciones que por diversas circunstancias había recibido la Iglesia, entre ellas aquélla que consideraba que, por derecho divino, la Iglesia tenía facultades para adquirir y poseer cualquier clase de bienes.

A pesar de que no eran propiamente un partido político, aunque Lucas Alamán considere que sí lo eran, es evidente que los conservadores que vivieron en las primeras décadas del México independiente tuvieron un programa de acción que los llevó a participar activamente en las asambleas parlamentarias, el gobierno municipal, los ministerios dependientes del poder Ejecutivo, el Supremo Poder Conservador y el Poder Ejecutivo mismo. El padre del conservadurismo, Edmund Burke, fue el primero que se dio cuenta de la eficacia del apoyo brindado por los medios de comunicación, ofrecidos por la moderna tecnología, a los divulgadores de las ideas libertarias y revolucionarias. Por eso postuló el contraataque organizado para socavar, a su vez, los postulados que surgían del triunfo de la Revolución francesa. Al panfleto había que responder con otro panfleto, y a la participación política había que enfrentarle la misma forma de acción.[10]

Ahora bien, ¿cuál era el límite de ese contraataque? En el caso concreto de México, el límite fue impuesto por la derrota militar y la presión económica, las cuales hicieron posible la separación de la Iglesia y el Estado. La derrota militar, tras la Guerra de Reforma, permitió dictar la legislación sobre la desamortización y la nacionalización de los bienes de la Iglesia. La desamortización cambió la correlación de fuerzas y dio lugar al surgimiento de una nueva clase propietaria que era laica y estaba constituida por personas físicas y no personas colectivas.

Por otra parte, la separación de la Iglesia y el Estado implicaba la secularización de todas aquellas instituciones en que había tenido ingerencia la Iglesia en la época colonial. Algunas de esas materias eran el control y registro del estado de las personas, la educación, la asistencia pública y, más que nada, el control de las conciencias. El origen último de la posición que asumieron los liberales en estas materias se encuentra en la política de los Borbones que buscaba constituir a la monarquía española como un estado nacional.

Si tuviéramos que elegir un texto mexicano en el que se condense el ideario conservador en forma concisa y clara, coincido con Jorge Adame en que este texto sería la obra de Clemente de Jesús Munguía: *Del Derecho Natural en sus principios comunes y en sus diversas ramificaciones, o sea, Curso elemental de Derecho Natural y de gentes, público, político, constitucional y principios de legislación,* publicado en 1849.[11] Ahí se encuentran claramente explicados todos los principios en que se debe basar la acción del hombre dentro de la sociedad, en todas las manifestaciones posibles: en su familia, con los demás hombres, frente al Estado, como funcionario o servidor público y, por último, con la Iglesia. Todo lo que escribe Munguía se basa en los principios perfectos e inmutables del derecho divino, de él se desprenden las leyes humanas que son las que sirven para regular la vida de los hombres. No por esto se crea que dicho texto es un simple catálogo de las obligaciones morales del hombre, sino que se trata de un tratado que abarca las más diversas materias contempladas a la luz del derecho natural.

Su utilidad es muy grande, ya que permite ver el alcance que para los conservadores tuvieron vocablos que en boca de los revolucionarios o simplemente de los liberales tenían un significado completamente distinto porque la base de que partían era otra. En ese caso se hallan los conceptos y alcance de la igualdad, la libertad, la propiedad, el sufragio, la representación, la ley, la sociedad civil y los derechos de la Iglesia.

Munguía era clérigo, y de ahí que estuviera obligado a difundir sus ideas conforme a la doctrina de la Iglesia. En este hecho radica precisamente su interés porque puede servir de parámetro para comparar su pensamiento con el que otros conservadores que no eran clérigos, aunque sí católicos por supuesto, externaron en su actuación como escritores, diputados, periodistas, miembros de alguna corporación, o abogados.

He elegido algunas ideas de dos conservadores mexicanos que se destacaron en la vida pública para mostrar su correspondencia o sus diferencias con las ideas de Munguía: Lucas Alamán y Juan N. Rodríguez de San Miguel. No se trata de hacer el análisis exegético del pensamiento de ninguno de los tres autores, simplemente de mostrar algunas de las ideas que permitirían confirmar si las hipótesis hasta aquí externadas son aceptables y eventualmente susceptibles de comprobación.

La primera diferencia que salta a la vista es que el pensamiento de Alamán encuentra su fuente de inspiración en Edmund Burke, señalado en este ensayo repetidas veces como el padre del conservadurismo.

El autor que inspira el pensamiento de Rodríguez de San Miguel también era inglés, pero nació mucho antes de la Revolución francesa: Francis Bacon. Fuera de este autor, Rodríguez sólo cita las Sagradas Escrituras o textos jurídicos. Olvidé señalar que era abogado. Por su parte, Munguía es un producto típico de la cultura mexicana de la época, a saber, sus citas son de lo más variadas, ya que incluye tanto los textos católicos como los que postulan doctrinas heterodoxas, pero para mantener su ideario.

Personalmente, me sentí sorprendida al ver las fuentes que inspiran el pensamiento de unos y otros. Pienso que Alamán eligió a Burke porque, de los tres autores mexicanos que cito, fue el único que vivió en su adolescencia la insurrección de 1810. Para Alamán debían tener un significado distinto los juicios emitidos por Burke sobre la Revolución, además, como aquél, Alamán fue un político práctico, combativo, que sabía dar dos pasos para atrás para consolidar uno para adelante. Munguía y Rodríguez estaban en su más tierna infancia cuando se produjo la insurrección y esto les hace ver la formación del nuevo Estado de manera diferente. El ideario de Alamán parece estar enfocado más hacia la restauración de lo que había sido el mejor momento de la Nueva España, aunque el retorno no fuera completo en el orden económico. Munguía y Rodríguez parecen más acomodados a la sociedad en transformación que les tocó vivir, y en todo caso sólo buscan el respeto de parte de ese pasado; esa parte implica definitivamente a la Iglesia.

Los tres son contrarios a las ideas de representación democrática, ya que no creen en la igualdad de los hombres dentro de la sociedad. Señalan que los distingue la función que desempeñan en ella, el interés que representan en su seno y su mayor o menor riqueza de pensamiento, ideales y bienes. Alamán, además de impracticable, considera a la democracia en México una ironía, y su implantación una "pretensión absurda" por falta de condiciones apropiadas.

Los tres coinciden en su concepto de seguridad, el cual se enfoca a la defensa de la propiedad tanto de particulares como de la Iglesia. La libre circulación de la riqueza tenía como límite los derechos de la Iglesia. También están de acuerdo en que la única forma de mantener la seguridad está en el establecimiento de una fuerza pública organizada de manera que afiance el orden y garantice la justicia, la cual significa para ellos dar a cada quien lo suyo. Son, por otro lado, renuentes a las novedades y propugnan por el respeto a las costumbres que se habían ido desarrollando paulatinamente y se hallaban arraigadas en los hombres. Ninguno era partidario del cambio social.

De los tres el único que alude claramente a los indios y no ambiguamente a las "clases más necesitadas" es Alamán, pero su pensamiento sobre ellos se inscribe en la línea proteccionista seguida por la Corona en América. Lo que para Alamán es espíritu proteccionista a la manera estatal española, para Munguía y Rodríguez es caridad cristiana en beneficio de las clases más necesitadas, a las cuales se sumaban los indios. Los tres creen firmemente que el único lazo de unión entre los mexicanos estaba en el mantenimiento de la unidad religiosa. Para Alamán esto es también lazo de unión con las otras naciones hispanoamericanas frente a los Estados Unidos del Norte.

La comparación podría extenderse y entre más ejemplos que trajéramos a cuento quedaría más claro que no es desacertado para analizar el pensamiento conservador partir de los principios de la religión católica y el modo en que estos principios se manifiestan en la constitución de la familia, la sociedad y el Estado. Por eso, cuando en las asambleas legislativas se enfrentan unos y otros para ver qué forma de gobierno ha de darse a la nación, qué alcance han de tener los derechos del hombre dentro de la sociedad, cómo se elaborarán los cuerpos jurídicos, quiénes podrán votar y ser votados, los conservadores propiamente dichos, se autoimponen como límite las doctrinas de la Iglesia católica. Muchos de los postulados conservadores fueron asumidos también por los liberales, pero las más de las veces impuestos por la realidad social que pretendían regular, aunque también por intereses personales. También muchos postulados liberales fueron admitidos por los conservadores, pero siempre en la medida que no se hallaran incluidos como "errores" en el seno de la doctrina católica. El catálogo más completo de este tipo de errores fue promulgado por Pío IX a través de la bula *Quanta Cura* en 1864. En este catálogo, que se conoce como *Sílabo*, vemos condenadas las principales tesis liberales sobre las relaciones de la Iglesia y el Estado, el matrimonio civil, la enseñanza laica y las doctrinas racionalistas y socialistas.[12] Muchas materias en que los reyes de la dinastía borbónica pudieron inmiscuirse les estuvieron vedadas a los gobiernos liberales, aunque sus miembros fueran católicos. La Iglesia y el Estado, que habían tenido a lo largo de 300 años fines convergentes respecto de los miembros de la sociedad, separaron formalmente sus destinos desde 1859. El estado nacional sólo podía constituirse sobre las cenizas de los derechos que la Iglesia había detentado a lo largo de varias centurias.

Este hecho no podía, en modo alguno, transformar de golpe la realidad de aquella sociedad abigarrada y compleja que se había dado en el virreinato de la Nueva España. El primer paso estaba dado, el siguiente sería la constitución del Estado a la luz de un credo individualista que, en el seno de la sociedad mexicana de la segunda mitad del siglo XIX, no podía ser igualitario. Los que no eran iguales, que seguían siendo más, se fueron quedando al margen y sólo varias décadas después hicieron oír su voz. Pero eso ya es otro asunto.

5

"Neither a borrower nor a lender be": Financial Constraints and the Treaty of Guadalupe Hidalgo

Barbara A. Tenenbaum

The treaty of Guadalupe Hidalgo, signed on February 2, 1848, by representatives from Mexico and the United States, officially ended the Mexican-American War. According to its provisions, the United States absorbed over one-half of formerly Mexican territory and established most of its permanent southern and western continental boundaries.[1] In exchange, the United States paid Mexico 15 million dollars in cash over a five-year period and agreed to pay the claims brought against the Mexican government by United States citizens.[2]

Contemporaries and the historians who followed them assumed that the Mexican representatives signed the treaty because they believed that Mexico lacked both the political unity and the funds necessary to continue the struggle. However, they remained unaware of the political realities and fiscal constraints which helped produce the treaty and Mexican acceptance of its painful terms.

When Mexico finally became independent from Spain in 1821, its new rulers confronted several crucial challenges to their establishment of an effective government. They had to regain authority over territory far away from Mexico City which had slipped out of royal control during the years from 1808 and 1821. Further, they had to convince landowners and merchants that their new government could provide a visible and effective administration to control local caciques and restore colonial order and safety. Finally they had to create a workable tax structure in order to support a government and the troops needed to maintain stability.

Widespread objections to colonial taxation had been one of the focal points in the movement for independence. In the period following the imperial reorganization known as the Bourbon Reforms, the Spanish Crown increased the total number of taxes from 39 in 1760 to 84 in 1790. It also created a highly profitable state monopoly on the production and sale of tobacco products, whose proceeds went directly to Spain. The number and diversity of taxes protected the Crown from undue dependence on any one source of revenue and required a great many royal administrators, thus bolstering imperial presence and authority. The new taxes also produced greatly increased sums for the Royal Treasury.[3]

After the death of King Charles III in 1788 and the outbreak of the French Revolution in 1789, Spain became embroiled in costly European wars and by 1795 began borrowing heavily from wealthy Mexicans.[4] Further drains on the treasury compelled the Spanish Crown to promulgate the Laws of Consolidation in 1804. These laws ordered colonial officials to sell all nonessential property of the Catholic Church at public auction and send the proceeds to Spain. In New Spain, where the Church used its resources to make loans, the decree provoked considerable outcry, but royal administrators nevertheless were able to send approximately 10 million pesos to the Crown to the ultimate benefit of invading Napoleonic troops.[5]

Although Spain rarely repaid its debts, prosperous Mexicans continued to lend their money voluntarily to the Crown until 1812, when the sum outstanding totalled more than 35 million pesos. After that year, the elite demanded written guarantees in return for their money. For example, in 1813, they agreed to lend to Viceroy Félix Calleja in exchange for the receipts from the collections of sales taxes, from the pulque revenue, the road tax, and the special wartime tax on food. Finally Calleja compromised and pledged to turn over one-half of the tax collections from Mexico City in order to obtain enough money to keep the tobacco monopoly, the gunpowder factory, and the mint in operation. In 1815, the sales tax had risen to 16 percent and the viceroy had established a forced lottery.[6]

By the time Mexico finally declared itself independent from Spain, the viceregal government could depend only on revenues from the universally detested tobacco monopoly. Since the new nation could not take advantage of its predecessor's successful and efficient fiscal structure, it would have to fashion a new one to provide for its needs without sacrificing too much of the new leaders' popularity. Unfortunately, the new leaders could not depend on the same kind of voluntary financial support from the elite it had given the colonial regime. Wealthy Mexicans were reluctant to make new loans for many reasons. The lengthy wars for independence led to a breakdown of both the mining and agricultural economies, and to a general scarcity of capital following the mass exodus of Spanish merchants after 1810. And although the elite governed Mexico, it had split into progressive and traditionalist wings, thereby prompting an extra dose of caution. Finally, although the new nation acknowledged colonial debts, it would take years to reimburse the elite for their financial sacrifices. Therefore, Mexican governments would have to prove their effectiveness before they could expect new internal loans.

The first Mexican government under Iturbide quickly lowered mining, sales, and trade taxes, and eliminated Indian tribute and other duties generally acknowledged as uncollectible. Less than four months after independence was declared, the Mexican government was unable to meet its daily expenses. After Iturbide fell in 1823, a Congress dominated by progressives adopted a federalist Constitution and fiscal structure. It decided that the new Republic would finance itself from taxes on international trade, collected at the ports in order to avoid reestablishing the hated colonial system of indirect taxes and monopolies.

Federalism, however, was expensive; it required duplicate administrations on national and state levels, and forced Congress to give the states taxes which yielded 40 percent of colonial revenue. In return, the states agreed to pay the National Treasury a fixed sum based on population (the *contingente*) and Congress gave it a new 15 percent surcharge on normal import duties (the *internación*).[7]

The new system needed time before it functioned effectively. To avoid the risk of alienating its supporters, the government declined to ask either the elite or the Church for loans. Instead, the Mexican Republic under President Guadalupe Victoria borrowed 32 million pesos from two British investment houses.[8] The two loans kept Mexico politically stable until 1827, the longest period of calm the Republic would experience until the Presidency of José Joaquín de Herrera in 1848.

When many British banking houses, including the two which had made the original loans to Mexico, collapsed, and the international economy went into a decline, Mexico's revenue from customs duties dropped from $8,049,399 in 1826-27 to $5,912,126 in 1827-28, a loss of over 2 million pesos to an income of $15,137,981.[9] As a result, the new nation was unable to meet the interest due British bondholders in October 1827, and defaulted on its payments.[10]

Mexico's suspension of debt payments in 1827 seriously hurt its position in the international economy, burdened the Treasury with ever-growing foreign obligations, and made further foreign loans impossible for the next 30 years. But the Mexican government still needed additional revenues to supplement tax collections because the new fiscal system failed to collect adequate revenues.

Since the Mexican government could not expect further foreign loans and divisions among the elite had widened because of the activities of highly politicized masonic lodges, the Treasury proposed to obtain the necessary funds by offering to pay high interest rates for short-term loans. It authorized the first major internal loan of 8 million pesos (to be made up of equal amounts of cash and credits recognized at 50-60 percent of face value) on November 21, 1827, just seven weeks after the default on the British debt. Five days later, on November 26, several deputies introduced a law in Congress calling for the expulsion of all Spanish-born residents from Mexico.[11]

Many Spaniards took advantage of this opportunity to demonstrate their loyalty to their new *patria* in cash, and in return, the government exempted them from the expulsion order and permitted them to stay in the country. Others, mostly merchants, also lent to the government, but because they were not under threat of expulsion, their motivations were exclusively financial.[12]

As the government's need for money increased, it offered ever more favorable terms, and a group of regular lenders sprang up willing to supply needed funds for short periods at high rates of interest. On December 24, 1827, the Treasury agreed to accept credits at more than 60 percent of their face value, and by the end of the year it had to enact a law prohibiting loans of less than 20 percent in cash.[13] Soon it began to settle debts with letters payable directly from tariff receipts for the total face value of the loan plus a monthly rate of interest, regardless of how much of the loan had been supplied in cash.

By the end of 1827, before any revolt had overthrown an elected government of the Mexican Republic, lending money to the government usually at high rates for short periods (*agiotaje*) had become an established and highly profitable business in Mexico. At the close of the 1827-28 fiscal year, the amount borrowed within the country had grown $755,936 (1633 percent) over the previous year. The amounts steadily increased in the years that followed.[14]

These internal loans helped pay for the army and the civil administration, but they did nothing to solve the problem of fiscal insufficiency. When the money derived from the British loans ran out, the political battle over control of the scarce resources that remained eventually led to revolts. These produced additional expenditures which diminished revenues still more. Thus, inadequate government revenues fostered insecurity and made the army anxious, unreliable, and rebellious. Fiscal weakness bred political instability, which further fueled fiscal weakness.

Frequent revolts and constant deficits added to elite reluctance to contribute to the national government either through loans or through more realistic tax programs. During the remainder of the first federalist period (1828-1834), Mexican politicians began to cite factionalism as the foremost problem facing the Republic. They attacked excessive expenditures as the key to deficits, rather than creating ways to supplement revenue sources that were manifestly insufficient. For example, they ignored the drastic decline in revenue produced by the tobacco monopoly and the consistent failure of the states to pay their *contingente* to the national government. They bypassed most issues concerned with supplementing income because these inevitably led to discussions of new taxes, which the elite would not support. Therefore, from 1828 to 1834, Mexican governments followed a politically expedient course and continued to pin their hopes on trade as the key to future prosperity. In the meantime, they waited for revenues to increase and blamed immediate problems on factionalism, rather than risk revolt sponsored by groups wealthy enough to buy army loyalty, but unwilling to pay more taxes.

As federalists and centralists blamed the other for the current fiscal catastrophes, *agiotaje* continued unabated. The government honored exorbitant interest rates, sometimes exceeding 300 percent per year, from its only consistent source of revenue—the customs receipts— from which it also expected to pay more than half of its operating expenses. Administrations in power spent the treasury of their successors, forcing them in turn to borrow still more. By 1830 the pattern was well-established as internal borrowing became a way of life, necessitated by the inadequate and inefficient revenue structure.

Mexican politicians knew that the fiscal system required serious adjustment and that *agiotaje* should not continue indefinitely. During the period from the default in October 1827 to the effective end of federalism in December 1834, they tried several different kinds of remedies. In 1829, Treasury Minister Lorenzo Zavala levied new taxes and Congress reduced all salaries and pensions for civil and military employees. Six weeks after Zavala had decreed the final group of new taxes, President Vicente Guerrero forced him to resign and repealed the new taxes.[15]

Shortly thereafter, the traditionalist sector of the elite supported a successful coup in December 1829, headed by General Anastasio Bustamante and directed by Lucas Alamán. They tried to solve the fiscal problem by reducing the deficit through better management and by renegotiating the British debt as a first step toward luring new foreign investment and loans to Mexico. Their strategy failed because foreign capitalists refused to lend and the new group of managers also had to borrow. In fact, the Bustamante administration added a new category to its 1830-31 budget report, "Borrowing in Anticipation of Customs Receipts."[16] The government began issuing letters on customs collections yet to be received. During its two years in office, the Bustamante administration listed approximately 4 million pesos in new internal debts under this one heading and borrowed a total of $2,356,997 (1830-31) and $3,734,566 (1831-32) from moneylenders.[17]

Its successors, Antonio López de Santa Anna and Valentín Gómez Farías, representing the federalist, progressive sector of the elite, tried to sell Church property and use the proceeds to pay government expenses. They hoped to use church wealth to save the federalist fiscal system, but their plan aroused so much hostility that the traditionalist sector of the elite convinced Santa Anna to remove Gómez Farías and his attack on Church wealth, and to abandon federalism instead. On December 8, 1834, the national government proclaimed its right to "confiscate state tax collections in order to pay the *contingente*" and in effect established a centralist government.[18]

Centralism was created to restore stability by satisfying four key groups. It rewarded the army by abolishing state militias, it pleased business interests which believed that a strong army guaranteed order and improved trade, it saved the Church, and it restored the traditionalist elite to power. Nevertheless, the centralist structure required that power emanate from a government in Mexico City strong enough and confident enough to maintain tight control over all the territory of the Republic.

Santa Anna and his supporters, however, had established the new system to bolster a weak government in Mexico City by draining the resources of the states (now renamed departments) for the benefit of the National Treasury. Their plan failed because Mexico was too vast, and communications and transportation too poor, for effective central control. Such difficulties surfaced when government troops were unable to crush rebels in Texas. Their failure to subdue that challenge to central authority undoubtedly encouraged others, prompted foreign invasion, and exposed the bankruptcy of centralist pretensions. Such conflicts reduced revenues while increasing expenditures.

Centralist leaders tried to bolster the system by decreeing forced loans on the Church, and when that failed, by levying taxes on urban property, rural property, and income in urban areas (*propiedades, rentas y giros*). These were the first new taxes to remain in effect since the beginning of the Republic. In 1838, the government tried to increase revenues by lowering customs duties by 10 percent to their 1821 levels. Subsequently, it added new imposts on property and individuals, and increased the *consumo* (the tax paid on imported goods purchased outside the ports) by 10 percent.[19]

The new centralist taxes might have contributed substantially to the Treasury had not other burdens—the Texas revolt, the Pastry War and subsequent indemnity to France, the pledge to settle claims owed to the United States in 1838-39, the suppression of revolts throughout the country—depleted resources far in excess of the Treasury's capacity to gather them. Therefore, governments consistently turned to the now ubiquitous moneylenders for additional funds.

The new Santanista administration also altered its relationship to the agiotistas. It acknowledged its inability to repay its obligations to all of the moneylenders and asserted its right to reimburse some in credits instead of cash. Later it issued "amortization credits" in four separate classes paying up to 30 percent in cash from the customs revenues and the remainder in credits (*vales de amortización*).[20] The new policy had very important consequences.

From 1827 to 1834 many people, particularly merchants active in the import-export trade who had ready access to cash, lent money to the government and became agiotistas. These transactions could be highly profitable. For example, in 1833 the merchant firm of Drusina and Martínez earned almost 25 percent of its profits from *agiotaje*.[21] However, when the government started paying debts in credits instead, the smaller lenders were forced out of business, since they no longer had any cash to lend. Consequently, governments fell increasingly into the hands of a small number of large-scale agiotistas.

After 1834, moneylenders often received payments well in excess of their cash outlay by using the new credits as part of the loan. In 1839, the government was desperate for funds because of the French blockade of Veracruz. In March it borrowed $140,000 in credits and $22,150 in cash from Francisco María Iturbe, Antonio Garay, Antonio Zurutuzu, and Hube and Company for a period of six months in exchange for $120,150 in letters on import duties (worth 58 percent and 68 percent of duties levied and $42,000 in letters on duties on the export of silver. The arrangement contained 86 percent in credits (purchased at 15 percent of their face value) and 14 percent in cash. In effect, the agiotista firms lent the government $140,000 in credits, costing them approximately $21,000 in cash, in exchange for guaranteed repayment of the full $140,000 in cash (a 666 percent profit on the credits).[22] In addition, the government reassured creditors by creating special funds from customs receipts to repay outstanding loans. The first such fund, which pledged 15 percent of customs to pay back loans, was created on January 20, 1836. The "Fifteen percent Fund," as it was known, gave priority to credits derived from agiotista loans and pledged that 85 percent of the full amount would be repaid in cash. By contrast, holders of other internal debt credits rarely received even 5 percent of customs. In fact, the "Fifteen percent" creditors received almost as much as the British bondholders, who by then were only entitled to 16.7 percent of the receipts from Veracruz and Tampico.[23]

When Anastasio Bustamante returned to the Presidency in 1839, new Treasury Minister Francisco Javier Echeverría, himself an agiotista, initiated a new policy. He paid fund creditors assiduously and, by 1840, both the "Fifteen" and the newly formed "Seventeen percent Fund" had been completely repaid. Many agiotistas made enormous profits—in 1840, Martínez del Río Hermanos held 9.8 percent of the firm's assets in debt credits, but these earned 44.9 percent of the firm's total gross profits for that year.[24]

Although the moneylenders flourished under this policy, it almost bankrupted the government. Treasury Minister Manuel María Canseco, Echeverría's successor, noted that although expenditures for the Treasury Ministry in 1840 totalled $12,484,047, they could be broken down into $2,375,314 for the Ministry's operating costs and $10,108,733 for repayment of loans.[25] Indeed, during the years from 1834 to 1844, treasury expenses consistently exceeded those for the military without exception, despite the fact that the nation was frequently at war or in revolt.[26] His careful repayment of agiotistas precipitated Bustamante's downfall and the rise of Santa Anna in December 1841.

Santa Anna's government tried diligently to improve the fiscal system. Although he began his term by slashing the Bustamante tax increases, Treasury Minister Ignacio Trigueros levied new ones on urban property, rural property, industrial plants, wages and salaries, professions and trades, luxuries, and a head tax of a half real per month.[27]

These taxes, combined with the others remaining from previous administrations, formed one of the most modern and progressive tax systems in the world in the nineteenth century. As such, it required a well-organized and efficient administration structure to assess and collect the new levies, an apparatus which Mexico still lacked. Nevertheless, centralism, particularly under Santa Anna from 1842 to 1844, created a fiscal system intended to serve the Treasury well, had not war intervened.

Despite efforts to improve national tax policy from 1842 until the outbreak of the war with the United States, both the government and the agiotistas suffered from the effects of the previous largesse. The prompt repayment of Creditors' Funds propelled many moneylenders into heavy speculations with debt paper in hopes of high returns. But in 1842, Santa Anna stopped payment to all existing Funds, transforming creditors into competitors because the Treasury could not repay all of its obligations in cash.

Foreign-born agiotistas and others with influence enlisted the aid of their respective ministries, while native Mexicans utilized deputies and senators and made alliances with each other to get their debts paid.[28] Many, like Martínez del Río Hermanos, Manning and MacKintosh, J. P. Penny and Company, and Montgomery, Nicod, and Company, went to British Minister Richard Pakenham for redress, who secured a separate Convention from Santa Anna to handle only debts owed to them. Soon thereafter Santa Anna stopped payment to this Convention and through more British mediation, it was included in the "Five percent Fund". But these maneuvers could hardly disguise the fact that the government needed to pay the agiotistas so that they could make more loans. The struggle over repayment simply winnowed the field once more, as had taken place in 1834.

The Treasury needed more revenue and so governments had to promise those remaining agiotistas some incentives in order to borrow in such uncertain times. The new loan cycle began in December 1844 when opposition leaders borrowed $500,000 to overthrow Santa Anna. The next administration tried to cut back on loans by announcing in March 1845 that contracts made during the previous administration would not be included in the capital of the loan to be repaid, except for contracts involving "items necessary for the public welfare such as uniforms, arms, etc." Thereafter the speculators hid behind the smokescreen of "necessary items."[29] In addition, Treasury Minister Luis de la Rosa borrowed 3 million pesos from the firm of Garruste and Company.[30]

In November 1844, the citizens of the United States elected James Knox Polk, the dark horse Democratic candidate, as President. His elevation to the Presidency strongly indicated that the United States would pursue the annexation of both Oregon and Texas, since he had pledged himself to that policy during the campaign. The incorporation of the independent Republic of Texas into the United States virtually assured war with Mexico.

From December 6, 1844, to June 20, 1848, twelve different governments "ruled" Mexico: Herrera, Paredes y Arrillaga, Bravo, Salas, Gómez Farías, Santa Anna, Anaya, Santa Anna, Peña y Peña, Anaya, Peña y Peña, and finally Herrera. During this chaotic period, no administration managed to decree or collect new taxes. In fact, declarations which hinted at future taxes only multiplied instability because they provoked revolts and made it impossible for agiotistas to do business. For example, just as Martínez del Río Hermanos concluded a deal with the first Herrera administration concerning the redemption of tobacco bonds, Herrera was overthrown by Paredes y Arrillaga. On May 2, 1846, Paredes suspended all Fund payments, and the agiotistas immediately went to British Minister Charles Bankhead. His efforts were frustrated by the announcement of a new accord on the British debt signed by the agiotista Manuel Escandón and the agiotista Ewen Clark MacKintosh, British consul in Mexico City and bondholder representative.[31] In the meantime, Paredes y Arrillaga declared war on the United States.

By the close of 1846, wealthy residents had contributed substantially to the war effort. On November 19, 1846, the government assigned parts of a 2 million peso loan to specific individuals; residents of the Federal District alone were responsible for $921,000. Of the $800,000 assessed at ranges of $5,000, $9,000, and $20,000 apiece, known moneylenders contributed at least $204,000.[32]

At the same time, the government looked to the Church for funds. In October 1846, Treasury Minister Antonio Haro y Tamariz devised a plan for clerical disentailment. Although the clergy refused to acquiesce in any such proposal, it did agree to lend the government $850,000 on December 5, 1846. A short time later, the Church lent another 1 million pesos.

Nevertheless, on January 11, 1847, Vice President Valentín Gómez Farías decreed the forced nationalization and sale of 15 million pesos' worth of Church property. The Church retaliated by convincing the national guard in Mexico City to stage the "revolt of the polkos" (so-called for their supposed allegiance to United States President

James Polk). Although the revolt failed to overthrow the government, it forced Santa Anna to return to Mexico City, repeal the law, and fire Gómez Farías in exchange for a $1.5 million loan guarantee.[33] However, the damage had already been done. In the preceding months, the government authorized loans of up to $20 million to be secured by specific pieces of Church property. Because the Archdiocese of Mexico City had little cash, it authorized the government to sell promissory notes and use Church property as collateral. Treasury Minister Juan Rondero and his cronies Gregorio Mier y Terán, Rosas Hermanos, Francisco Iturbe and others were able to choose their properties and pay 50 percent in cash and 50 percent in bonds. To raise still more money, the clergy also had to sell $1.2 million of preindependence debt credits at 8 percent of face value and then turn over the $96,000 to the government. The purchasers, among whom was Ewen MacKintosh, then used the credits to form other loans.[34]

The Church had considerable difficulty repaying purchasers of treasury bills in cash and often had to borrow from some moneylenders to pay off others. Eventually, the Church had to sell 16 properties in downtown Mexico City at two-thirds of their assessed value to the agiotista Gregorio Mier y Terán.[35] In response to clerical pleas, the government repealed a law prohibiting the Church from demanding the immediate repayment of its loans to urban and rural property holders. In exchange, the government received money from the Bishop of Michoacán to purchase muskets.[36]

Although the Treasury borrowed money at a frantic pace, the war did not seriously jeopardize tax collections from July 1845, when General Zachary Taylor's army crossed the Nueces River, until the landing of General Winfield Scott's forces in Veracruz on March 9, 1847. Up until Scott's invasion and its accompanying naval blockade of virtually the entire Gulf coast, the war affected frontier areas like Nuevo México, California, and certain northern states. Its army occupied only Tampico and ventured south into Mexico only as far as Saltillo and Chihuahua.[37]

According to the meticulously detailed Treasury Report for 1844, the centralist revenue structure primarily depended on collections from nine departments. Until March 29, 1847, the National Treasury continued to receive revenues from eight of them unimpeded by enemy forces. Scott's occupation of Veracruz, however, posed serious problems. In 1844, the department of Veracruz collected $5,933,105 in taxes, or 19 percent of the total gross income of $31,873,019 for the nation.[38] With that and the revenue from the customs houses of

Tampico and Matamoros gone, the Mexican government was much less able to prosecute the war. After Puebla was occupied on May 15, the Treasury lost another million pesos. Finally, when Scott conquered and occupied Mexico City in late August, the government lost the revenue from its wealthiest state. Furthermore, Scott proceeded to levy a monthly tribute on the capital of $150,000 and abolished the sales tax (*alcabala*), its major source of income.[39]

But Mexico could still have continued its war effort. For example, in 1864 and 1865, French troops pushed Juárez and his forces to the United States border. At that time, the invaders had a much stronger hold over the country than Scott had had in 1847 and controlled virtually every revenue source in the Republic. Nevertheless, two years later, Juárez's forces, aided by a French withdrawal, reconquered the Mexican nation.

In 1847, despite the lack of unanimity among the various factions, several groups of leaders were ready to continue the war and force United States troops to occupy the entire country before surrendering. Yet, in what seems like indecent haste by Mexican standards, the national government, headed by a group of *moderados*, made peace and signed the Treaty of Guadalupe Hidalgo, losing one-half of its national territory in the process.

Scholars generally credit the signing of the treaty to the persistence and sagacity of the chief negotiator for the United States, Nicholas P. Trist, then Chief Clerk of the U.S. State Department. In reality, however, it appears that the Catholic Church, the agiotistas, and the British diplomatic corps played important roles in attaining that objective.

The letters Trist sent to his superior, U.S. Secretary of State James Buchanan, shortly after his arrival in Mexico in May 1847 indicate that he had little awareness of the existence of powerful moneylenders, their ties to the foreign ministries in the capital, and their influence over the Mexican government. Had he been aware of such interconnections, he might have been more wary of contacting British Minister Charles Bankhead on June 6 to deliver messages to the Mexican government. Yet, British involvement would prove decisive in the ultimate success of the negotiations and final signing of a treaty. Instead, Trist was very grateful that Minister Bankhead had agreed to facilitate matters and had assigned his junior, Edward Thornton, to assist him.

Historians of the war on both sides have been unaware of Thornton's prior involvement in agiotista disputes, particularly those involving the Martínez del Río family. For example, less than two weeks after Trist wrote to Bankhead, that company went to Thornton to assist it in reducing its $2,250 assessment in the most recent forced loan. When a group of soldiers appeared at the firm's headquarters with orders to embargo the company and seize its assets on July 21, 1847, Thornton came to the rescue and the troops departed. Eventually, British Foreign Minister Lord-Palmerston won an exemption for the firm.[40] Furthermore, Thornton worked closely with the British consul in Mexico City, Ewen Clark MacKintosh, one of the most prominent agiotistas and the representative of the British bondholders. With sources such as these so close to the negotiations, the entire agiotista community in the capital was kept informed of the status of the talks and the amount of money involved.

Although analysts have been quick to note Mexico's financial difficulties as one of the main motivations for its capitulation, they have been unaware of the more subtle manifestations of agiotista pressure. And the British, too, were hardly disinterested parties. They had two substantial reasons for facilitating Trist's treaty-making. The promised United States indemnity payments to Mexico would help pay debts still outstanding since 1827 to British bondholders. It would also provide the means of reimbursing agiotistas and thus resolving troublesome claims on the Mexican government and on the British representatives' time and energy. British consul MacKintosh had additional motives for helping matters along, since he stood to profit considerably as agent for the bondholders and as one of those who would convert dollars paid in the United States into pesos paid to the government in Mexico City.[41] Trist knew other agiotistas as well; his correspondence mentions Luis Hargous, Lionel Davison, and Guillermo de Drusina.[42]

Conversely, Trist was well aware of the clergy's eagerness to make peace. In fact, Trist wrote to Buchanan that the upper clergy advocated that the United States absorb Mexico in order to preserve its possessions.[43] In the period prior to the Reform, the Church still had much to lose were the war to continue.

But it was the agiotistas' influence, and not the clerics', which won the day. On July 3, Luis Hargous wrote to Thornton that he had suggested to Trist that he should "[make] use of money in Mexico for what I mentioned to you [bribing various government officials] and urged him to support this course to General Scott."[44] By July 16, Trist was convinced and wrote Scott that "the only way in which the indefinite protraction of this war can possibly by prevented . . . is by the secret expenditure of money at the city of Mexico . . . the only alternative is an early movement upon the capital."[45] Scott agreed, noting that "the occupation by the U.S. forces of twenty of the principal places in this Republic in addition to those already in our hands, would not probably, in a year or more force the Mexican authorities to sue for, or to accept a peace on any terms honourable or just to our country without bribes."[46]

By the end of July, MacKintosh had become a clandestine intermediary between Trist and Santa Anna, with Thornton acting as messenger. As the American troops marched toward Mexico City in August, Foreign Minister José Ramón Pacheco sent an unsealed note through Thornton to Trist, addressed to U.S. Secretary of State Buchanan, asking for peace. During discussions beginning on August 30, 1847, Trist indicated to Santa Anna through intermediaries that he could guarantee that the "Mexican government (could) convert the entire amount (of the United States indemnity) into cash, without loss and probably at a considerable premium, immediately upon the exchange of ratifications." He noted that he was "much encouraged by the effect produced by this intimation . . . (his) expectations were evidently far exceeded by the amount named." Trist added that the intermediary had a "very deep stake" in making a peace for business reasons and "had a very well grounded expectation that he would be profitably concerned in the management and disposal of the stock to be issued by our government."[47] Trist's description of this valuable go-between easily fits with our knowledge of MacKintosh and his role in Mexican affairs. But negotiations broke down, Scott's army conquered Mexico City, and Santa Anna's government collapsed.

In the meantime, President Polk had grown increasingly impatient over Trist's failure to produce a treaty, and ordered Secretary of State Buchanan on October 5 to write to his subordinate, demanding his immediate return to Washington. President Polk's decision to recall him created innumerable difficulties for Trist, however, and almost denied the United States the treaty it sought so urgently. Just as Trist received his recall orders, he was advised that a new Mexican political party (*moderados*) had been formed with the express purpose of making peace. As Trist wrote to Buchanan, "this party cannot possibly stand, unless the object for which alone it had been formed itself be speedily accomplished."[48] In other words, he had to make peace soon.

The British encouraged Trist in this view. When Thornton delivered a message to Trist from Ministro de Relaciones Peña y Peña on the appointment of a new peace commission on November 22, the

English diplomat added that he thought this event signalled that the Mexicans wanted to make peace.[49] Yet, Trist had been recalled and had to leave Mexico immediately.

Although there is little evidence in Trist's correspondence of British efforts to keep him in Mexico, he quickly became convinced that he must stay. On November 28, he wrote his wife, Virginia, advising her that he planned to "bid adieu forever to official life" and hoped to leave Washington and settle with her and the family in Westchester County, New York. And on December 4, he wrote once more and told her that he was determined to stay in Mexico and "make a treaty if it can be done."[50] Thornton was delighted and wrote Trist that "once full information arrived in Washington, the administration would applaud the decision."[51]

While Trist was convinced that the Mexicans were preparing to negotiate, the official representatives were still waiting for the government in Querétaro to instruct them on their position prior to the talks. One of the commissioners, Miguel Atristain, described by Ramón Alcáraz as "MacKintosh's lawyer," rode to Querétaro and returned quickly with the necessary orders.[52] Nevertheless, negotiations proceeded slowly, particularly over the Mexicans' demand for $30 million instead of the 15 million Trist was prepared to offer. Finally, in late January, Trist threatened to end the talks altogether.[53]

At this point, Percy Doyle, Bankhead's successor as British Minister, personally entered the fray, despite his previous pledges to remain uninvolved. First, he persuaded Trist to refrain from hasty action. Next, he personally travelled to Querétaro and met with the leaders of the interim government. The records indicate that he told them that the United States troops under General Scott would protect them should revolt break out after the treaty was signed, despite the fact that, as British Minister, he had no authority to make such a promise. Therefore, it seems reasonable to assume that he also reminded them of Mexican obligations to bondholders in Britain and to agiotistas in Mexico.[54] On February 2, the treaty was signed.

Many politicians in the United States were aware of British participation in the making of the treaty, although they did not discuss their pecuniary interests in the matter. Sam Houston even cited British involvement as one of the reasons why Congress should reject the treaty.[55] Nevertheless, without British assistance, it seems likely that the United States would not have obtained so much territory at such a modest price. Had Trist returned home when his recall orders arrived, it is doubtful that the Mexicans and the Americans would have arrived at any agreement. Rather, the *moderados* would have fallen and those advocating a protracted guerrilla war would have held the upper hand, perhaps until the candidate of the antiwar Whigs, Zachary Taylor, was elected President of the United States in November.

The treaty of Guadalupe Hidalgo had many unanticipated consequences that affected all of the interested parties. In the short term, MacKintosh fared the best and Trist, the worst. The British moneylender received $600,000 from the first $3 million installment paid from the United States indemnity to Mexico to reimburse an undocumented loan made to Treasury Minister Juan Rondero in July 1847. But when called upon to present the 5 million pesos worth of tobacco credits which the government had used as collateral for the loan, he was only able to produce half the amount. He also made $179,960 and $146,470 in commissions when he converted indemnity dollars into pesos in 1849 and 1851, respectively. And, of course, he earned an additional commission when the Mexican government renegotiated the British debt and paid the bondholders 2.5 million pesos. Yet, he grew overconfident with these successes, and went bankrupt in 1850 due to compulsive overspeculation.[56]

Nicholas P. Trist, conversely, received little praise for the treaty for which he had worked so hard. Polk was outraged by Trist's behavior and angrily condemned him as an "imprudent and unqualified scoundrel."[57] Nevertheless, he urged ratification of the treaty simply because it ended a war which had already outlived its popularity. Southerners like Sam Houston, on the other hand, argued for its rejection because its territorial gains were too limited, while others complained that the new lands were too vast.[58] Trist never received the applause of a grateful administration as Thornton had predicted, and he quietly retired into obscurity.

Mexico, which emerged from the war greatly reduced in size, changed as a result of the experience. The pain of invasion led to a new and more sophisticated understanding of the political and social problems confronting the nation, and the indemnity funds paid for four years of peace. The quiet years of federalism under Presidents José Joaquín de Herrera and Mariano Arista, the first since Guadalupe Victoria in 1824–1828, enabled a new generation of liberal leaders to gain some practical experience and stature. Such men as Benito Juárez and Melchor Ocampo became the governors of their states; Guillermo Prieto, Manuel Payno, and Ocampo became Treasury Ministers; and Ignacio Comonfort headed the customs at Acapulco.

Their increased knowledge of government helped create and sustain the Reform movement.

The United States, of course, benefited substantially from the Treaty of Guadalupe Hidalgo. It received immensely valuable land, incorporated overnight thousands of Mexicans with their distinctive culture and traditions, and established a generally peaceful boundary with its southern neighbor. But the great expansion of territory inevitably aggravated existing sectional disputes and propelled the United States into the most costly struggle in its history, the Civil War.

6

Patriarchy and the Status of Women in the Late Nineteenth-Century Southwest

Richard Griswold del Castillo

Even before the widespread urban and industrial transformations of the twentieth century, the ideology and value system associated with the Mexican patriarchal family was hardly a monolithic one. The traditions of the juridical protection of women's rights, the emergence of romantic love, the necessity for frontier egalitarianism, and the idealization of certain female roles outside the home were themes which had their origin in pre-American times. Moreover, demographic and economic patterns which intensified in the post-1848 period made it increasingly difficult for Mexican Americans to establish forms of family life which they preferred. A central thesis of this essay, and one that my book treats in more detail, is that the nineteenth-century Mexican-American family was characterized by a disparity between their familial ideals and day-to-day reality. This essay then explores the ideology of patriarchy as it developed in previous eras in Spain and Mexico. The last portion describes the economic and demographic pressures that beset the majority of Mexican Americans making patriarchal family life much more an ideal than a reality.[1]

The Historical Development of Patriarchal Ideologies

During the nineteenth century, most upper- and middle-class Mexican Americans in the Southwest and Mexico shared a common set of expectations about the nature and degree of authority that was owed to the male head of the household. Sylvia Marina Arrom, describing the status of women in Mexico City during the early nineteenth century, summarized this patriarchal ideal as follows:

... the *pater familias* exercised his authority without restraints, unencumbered by tradition or competing power; he completely controlled his wife's legal acts, property and person, being able to claim her domestic services, obedience and sexual fidelity (although the double standard granted him sexual freedom); he made all important decisions to enforce his will upon its members using whatever means he deemed necessary.[2]

Ramón Gutiérrez, in his history of changing patterns of marriage in New Mexico in the seventeenth through the nineteenth centuries, has analyzed the concept of honor in relation to male authority within the family and argued that the patriarchal ideal had deep roots in Spanish racist ideology based on religion. The desire to maintain racial and thereby religious purity (*limpieza de sangre*) lay at the root of patriarchy. The wide-ranging powers of the father and husband were seen as necessary to protect the family, particularly the women, from what they considered pollution, corruption, and shame.[3]

Female honor, not just in Spain, but in other Mediterranean communities, was historically related to the social class system. Different codes of female sexual behavior were thought to be appropriate for different levels of the class hierarchy, with the aristocracy placing the greatest emphasis on female virtue. Reviewing the evidence for nineteenth-century Cuba, Verena Martínez-Alier concluded that, while not all hierarchical societies emphasized female purity, "... where there is such an emphasis, this is generally related to the existence of status groups."[4]

From Spanish colonial times, the Church and State, which sought to preserve the structured order of society, supported paternal authority. On the Mexican northern frontier in the early nineteenth century, more egalitarian relationships seem to have emerged as a result of increased trade between Mexico and the United States, as well as the common poverty endured by frontier families. No doubt, the sexual division of labor was more difficult to maintain in a society where everyone had to work to survive in a harsh environment. The divisions in sex roles were more rigid in wealthier, higher-status families because within these families women could be liberated from doing men's work. Among the majority of frontier families, however, men and women tended to share the labor of farming, ranching, and household chores.[5] The key to patriarchal values within the family lay not in the division of labor, but more in the authority given to the parents, especially to fathers. Ideally, the parents exerted their greatest authority in the selection of marriage partners for their children. Honor, status, property, and family ties were considered to be more important than considerations of romantic love.

Yet even this prerogative was eroding well before the American period began. In New Mexico, notions of romantic love and individual choice in marriage began to supplant parental control as early as 1600.[6] While attributing these changes in New Mexico primarily to increased capitalist activity, Gutiérrez emphasized that the seeds of romantic love and freedom from patriarchal controls in mate selection were present in Spanish and Mexican culture long before the rise of modern economic activity. The Catholic Church's official doctrine was that all souls were equal before God, and both the Church and State in colonial Mexico recognized grounds for divorce while maintaining the legal identity of women.[7]

In supporting parental authority, the Church and State helped to maintain patriarchy. Often, the authority of the parents to control their children was linked to religion. Respect for elders was cited in Scripture and Church doctrines and, on the family level, children were socialized to look on parents as having religious authority. In New Mexico, for example, the Abeyta family strove to perpetuate the authority of the elders by preparing lengthy written instructions for their children. These lessons, passed from generation to generation, served as a guide for perpetuating a family ideology. In the lesson book, the father was seen as imparting moral authority. He was the family priest, dispensing moral lessons and interpreting the word of God. A sample from the manuscript conveys the tone of the lessons:

> I have seen, Lord, your work and I have prostrated myself in your presence because your work sings your wisdom and your Justice. I have turned my eyes to man's work and I have muffled myself in dejection because their work proclaims their ignorance and their evil.[8]

In Tucson, families were sometimes led by the father or oldest member of the household in morning or evening prayers. Many families had special prayers that had been passed on through the generations. Carmen Lucero remembered that her family "got up at daylight and, led by the oldest member of the family, said family prayers and sang the 'Alba' or morning song."[9] Francisca Solano León remembered that her father regularly led the family in evening prayers; "no matter how tired he was, or we were, he had us all together, and we knelt down and said our rosary."[10]

Religious authority within the family was a cornerstone for patriarchal control; it extended beyond the immediate household, even to married children. José Arnaz, a californio recalled that it was not unusual for "an aged father to whip a married son with children and for his son to receive his lashes on his knees with a bowed head."[11] Another californio, Antonio Coronel, recorded that "the rule for the family was to particularly preserve respect for the head of the household, in the extreme a son or daughter, although married, was to submit to the orders of the parent."[12]

The Church sought to reinforce discipline within the family by its teachings. One example was a marriage manual, *La familia regulada*, that was in the library of Antonio Coronel, a Los Angeles ranchero.[13] It cited scriptural justifications for newly married couples to live apart from their parents, yet "the father-in-law, mother-in-law and other elders ought always to be listened to and respected by young people." And a married woman should "have special care to obey, help, and be courteous to the parents of her husband." Of all the evils that might infect a marriage, jealousy was the most dangerous and it was most likely to afflict women. "A poor woman possessed with jealousy does not rest during the day or night . . ." which may result in "the ruin of homes, the wasting of money, the loss of children, the scandal of servants, the bad example to the community, and, above all, the loss of souls."[14]

An important aspect of the ideal of patriarchal authority involved the subordinate position of women. In the Iberian Catholic and the pre-Columbian traditions, women were supposed to accept absolute male authority in the household. Spanish laws, including the *Siete Partidas*, frequently described the relationship between husband and wife in monarchical terms: "the husband is, as it were, the Lord and Head of his wife." Men were the "rulers," women the "subjects"; husbands were the "absolute monarchs" of the "nation" of the family.[15] During the first half of the nineteenth century, some Mexican authors idealized the subordination of women. Sylvia Marina Arrom, reviewing the legal handbooks, didactical tracts, and popular literature of that era concluded: "Throughout this literature women's primary functions in society were regarded as those of wife and mother."[16]

In New Mexico and elsewhere on the frontier, a code of honor dictated that men should act as guardians of the purity of the female family members. Gutiérrez summarized the sexual basis of this ideal for colonial New Mexico:

> Because nature created woman the weaker of the sexes and rendered her helpless to the whims and sexual desires of men, male authority over them was the only means by which shame and the family's honor could be guaranteed.[17]

In California, Ignacio Coronel considered the origin of women's status as having biblical foundations. Undoubtedly, the Church and his peers supported him in his views. In the 1860s he wrote: "The first woman (Eve) did not have any rivals; nevertheless, she wanted to obtain the apple; and ever since then, in a spirit of imitation, women have not ceased to accuse one another of this desire. . . . Man born before woman is thus more noble than she."[18] Accordingly, the sexual vulnerability of women dictated that they be closely cloistered within the home. Contacts between unmarried adults of the opposite sex had to be closely watched.

Kathleen Gonzales, who observed Mexican families in San Antonio during the 1920s, noted the persistence of a rigid male authority over women. She wrote that he "dictates to his wife what she is to do at all times and in all matters, their friends, dress and many other personal matters are approved or disapproved by her husband."[19] Ideally, the husband's authority was never to be resented by the wife, for she accepted the idea of her inferiority. In Gonzales's words, "Reared with the idea that she is inferior to men, she rather likes to be ruled. Since there is little else to hope for, she had dreamed since childhood of home and a husband."[20] In general, the women, married and unmarried, were prescribed to live within a restricted world of custom and restraint.

A strict separation of male and female roles within the family did not mean, however, that the wife lacked influence over household matters, especially in the rearing of the children. The ideal wife and mother was supposed to be primarily concerned with the management of the *casa* (home), and the husband was expected to defer to her in mundane domestic matters. His sphere of responsibility lay outside the home as a protector and breadwinner.

Exceptions to the Patriarchal Ideal

The ideals encompassed in the patriarchal tradition were often contradicted by the circumstances of day-to-day life. In central Mexico, women's position varied according to the socioeconomic status of their families, with wealthy women having relatively more freedoms than the poorer. The Spanish legal system, intent on guarding property, family honor, and *limpieza de sangre* gave women a number of rights which made them juridically equal to men. Women could inherit property and titles, testify in court, and sign contracts. Spanish laws gave married women the right to limit their husband's control of their dowry and single women, especially widows had a good deal of economic independence supported by the law. Throughout the colonial period, women could be found active outside the home in businesses, sharing ownership and management obligations with their husbands or as independent entrepreneurs. This was true for both the upper and lower classes.

Colin MacLachlan and Jaime Rodríguez, while finding that colonial Mexican society was patriarchal and that "once expelled from the protective network of the family, women had no place in decent society," concluded that Mexican women probably had more legal rights than elsewhere in the world. In their view:

> Spanish law was progressive and more cognizant of women's rights than most legal systems. As a result, colonial Mexican women enjoyed more rewarding lives than most of their contemporaries in other parts of the world.[21]

While this may have been true in the seventeenth century, it became less true "as Mexican society evolved social mores and legal restrictions circumscribed women's roles."[22] In the nineteenth century, Mexican legislators adopted the Napoleonic code which severely restricted women's rights and patriarchy found new support.

Mexican and Mexican-American history is full of examples of women who deviated from the submissive ideal. The first novel written in the New World, *La Monia Alferez,* was based on the real life story of Doña Catalina de Erazu, a renegade nun in colonial times who became a famous sword fighter and muleteer (*arriero*).[23] Mexican authors have produced hundreds of historical biographies of famous and heroic women. A rich folklore and literature have emerged around such women as Doña Marina or La Malinche, Cortes's mistress; Sor Juana Inés de la Cruz, a nun who was an outstanding poet in colonial times; Doña Josefa Ortiz de Domínguez or *La Corregidora,* a heroine of the Wars of Independence; and Las Soldaderas, the women who fought in the Mexican Revolution of 1910.[24]

On the Spanish and Mexican frontiers, there were scores of lesser-known women who were historically prominent exceptions to the patriarchal ideal. In the 1770s, María Feliciana Arballo y Gutiérrez, a rugged widow, accompanied De Anza on his second expedition to California. Doña Eulalia Fages, spirited wife of the governor of California in the 1780s, apparently influenced the political history of the province. In the 1820s, Doña Josefa Becerra, the wife of the Spanish governor of Texas, drilled troops and debated politics with the pueblo government during her husband's absence. Juana Birones de Miranda was one of 60 California women who managed, through their determined efforts, to obtain Mexican land grants prior to 1848.[25]

The pattern of these biographies suggests that there were socially acceptable ways in which women, particularly those of the upper classes, could act outside the rigid limits of the patriarchal family. In reality, women's roles were not always circumscribed by family obligations.[26] In colonial times, there was limited social support and even an idealization of certain kinds of female involvement beyond the confines of *la casa*. Most often nuns and aristocratic women, esteemed as model women, managed to achieve fame and influence in nontraditional ways.

The Mexican Wars of Independence and the chaotic years of the Mexican Republic (1821-1848) did much to liberate women and challenge older patriarchal values. The displacement of large masses of the population by war, famine, and political turmoil increased the likelihood that women would be active in nondomestic arenas. Currents of revolutionary egalitarianism from Europe and the United States tended to increase the acceptability of romantic love in personal relations and to weaken the importance of monarchical imagery in marriage.[27]

On the frontier, women and men worked and fought side by side out of necessity. A chronic scarcity of marriageable non-Indian women increased the bargaining power of Spanish and mestizo women, especially those who were emigrants from central Mexico. In New Mexico, after the 1770s, higher rates of illegitimacy and an increasing equality in the ages of marriage partners demonstrate the weakening of parental controls. Among the New Mexican aristocracy, and even among the lower classes, intermarriage and concubinage with foreigners increased, representing a loosening of the mechanisms of social control. The traditions of patriarchal authority, respect for elders, and female subordination did not disappear, however, but coexisted with new notions of romantic love and individualism.[28]

In California, the ideology of patriarchy seems to have undergone significant erosion during the gold rush years due to increased economic opportunities which drew many young adults away from their families and introduced them to new ways of life. The gold rush immigrations resulted in increased violence, gambling, drunkenness, and prostitution. It is little wonder the californios frequently complained that all this was destroying their older ways of life. The social ambience and sudden wealth of these early years of the American era made it increasingly difficult for parents to control their children.[29]

Patriarchy and Household Structure

Data on household organization in the urban Southwest provide a means of measuring deviations from the ideals of patriarchy during the late nineteenth century. Since male dominance within the household depended on the subordination of women and children, it is instructive to analyze the changing patterns of households where women were relatively independent of men. Table 1 illustrates variations in the proportions of female-headed households in Los Angeles, Tucson, Santa Fe, and San Antonio. With the exception of San Antonio, all the urban areas showed increases in matriarchal (female-headed) households during the thirty-year period 1850–80 (see Table 1). By 1880, in all towns, more than 25 percent of all Spanish surnamed households were headed by women. By this time, there was little geographical variation in the distribution.

TABLE 1

The Percentage of Female-Headed Households Among
Mexican Americans in Four Southwestern Towns

	Los Angeles	*Tucson*	*Santa Fe*	*San Antonio*
1850	28.9	–	25.9	36.7
1860	27.4	–	28.4	30.6
1870	37.7	17.6	31.7	33.9
1880	31.1	33.1	27.0	28.8

Barbara Laslett, in her study of extended households in 1850 in Los Angeles, found that females were more likely than men to be the head of augmented families, i.e., those that had relatives and others as members. She explained this pattern by noting that California's community property laws guaranteed married women the resources (land) to maintain extended families. Laslett hypothesized that children and older relatives were willing to stay in female-headed homes because of ties of affection as well as the authority the promise of land ownership conferred on the mother.[30] By 1870, however, this situation had changed so that women were more likely to head nuclear families with children. This Laslett attributed to shifts in women's job opportunities; as women's access to wealth, through property and paid labor, constricted, so, too, did their ability to maintain extended households.[31] A review of the data on female employment patterns, specifically the employment of female heads of household, indicates that this explanation is only partially true. Employment among female heads of household in all four southwestern towns increased after 1860, as did the prevalence of matriarchy among Mexican Americans elsewhere in the urban areas of the Southwest.

The closest comparison to the pattern of matriarchal families among Mexican Americans is the social history of the black family in the nineteenth century. Various researchers, using federal census data, have found higher percentages of black female-headed households than in European immigrant groups. For example, in 1880, 30 percent of black families in Atlanta, Georgia, were matriarchal. From 1850 to 1880, in seven cities along the Ohio River, the percentage of black female-headed families ranged from 27 to 30 percent. United States census figures from 1900 to the present continue to report higher incidences of female-headed households among blacks than among European immigrant groups.[32]

Revisionist historians argue that the institution of slavery did not destroy the black nuclear family and cause these high rates of matriarchy. Rather, they point to the effects of persistent poverty. Indeed, most black families before and after 1865 continued to be two-parent households as Herbert Gutman and Elizabeth Pleck have pointed out.[33] Gutman found that the matriarchal black family was more common in urban areas and that "most of these father-absent households were the result of the deaths of husbands and the surplus of adult black women to men." The percentages of female-headed households in the urban southern towns of Mobile, Richmond, Beaufort, and Natchez ranged from 26 to 31 percent of all black households.[34]

There were some immigrant groups, however, whose experience with female-headed households duplicated that of Mexican Americans and blacks. Laurence Glasco found that, in 1855, about 25 percent of Irish immigrant women who were not living with a husband were heads of separate households in Buffalo, New York.[35] When random samples of families are compared, while controlling for economic class, much of the difference in matriarchy by race, national origin, or ethnicity disappears. Among the urban poor, especially those who were immigrants or migrants from rural areas, unemployment and the difficulties and temptations of urban life seem to have been a primary cause of the breakup of nuclear families.[36]

Regardless of the shifts in real and potential wealth among Mexican American women, they were far from trapped within the confines of a male-dominated family. As heads of their own households, they were relatively independent of male supervision, even if their husbands were only temporarily absent.

TABLE 2

The Percentage of Males, Ages 20-59, Unemployed Among Mexican Americans

	Los Angeles	Tucson	Santa Fe	San Antonio
1850	23.0	—	15.9	15.3
1860	6.7	—	23.2	19.7
1870	12.3	13.9	26.0	22.3
1880	11.4	19.2	10.3	10.4

Declining job opportunities probably caused many married men to leave their families to look for work. Thus, the rates of unemployment for men are roughly correlated with the patterns of female-headed families in the four urban towns (see Table 2).[37] The types of jobs available to Mexican-American men kept them away from their families for long periods of time. *Arrieros* or teamsters, cartmen, wagon drivers, and drovers, as well as miners, vaqueros, and farm workers could expect, by the nature of their occupation, to be periodically absent from their families. Day laborers might have to migrate long distances to find work, leaving their families behind until they succeeded in establishing a new residence.

A prime example of this was the case of the Mexican miners in southern Arizona in the 1880s. The introduction of mechanization in the gold, silver, and copper mines forced hundreds of men out of work. Many of them opted to go "placering" along the Gila and Colorado Rivers.[38] The entrance of the railroads into the Southwest in the 1870s and 1880s disrupted the patterns of work for hundreds of *arrieros*. Many men left their families to search out short hauling contracts in areas not yet served by the railroad or to search for new jobs. Thus, the marginalization of the work force had a direct impact on family life.

Evidence from Los Angeles in the nineteenth century indicates that differential mortality rates also may have affected the incidence of female-headed households. During the period 1877-87, men in the prime age groups, 20 to 40 years of age, had a death rate almost twice that of females.[39] The dangers associated with mining and construction work probably created many widows elsewhere in the Southwest. But abandonments, both temporary and permanent, were a more frequent cause of the rising incidence of female-headed families. This, of course, was intimately bound to the changing nature of the economy. In 1864, María Josefa Bandini de Carrillo, a member of a landholding family in Santa Barbara, described the hard times which had forced members of her family to leave home to look for work. "We cannot live here," she wrote. "There are days upon days that we spend without eating, and without hope of leaving here." She related how her brothers finally set out as migrant workers. "I believe that they will first go to Los Angeles and, if they do not find work, they will go to San Francisco, more to the north."[40] But things were not much better for the californios in northern California. In 1869, Mariano Vallejo, a ranchero who had once been wealthy, explained he was forced to consider leaving California to seek work in Mexico "not because I want to, but out of necessity. I must earn a livelihood and meet my obligations as a father and provider."[41]

One example of how economic necessity forced the temporary absence of husbands from their wives and children is the example of James Tafolla in South Texas. Born in 1837 in Santa Fe and orphaned at a young age, James's first wife died shortly after he was married. In his second marriage, he supported his mother-in-law and one child. After a few years, a shortage of work forced him to leave home for several months. He traveled across the border to Mexico, where he found work with his brother-in-law. After a period of more than half a year, he returned to Texas with a small stake.[42]

Experiences like that of James Tafolla undoubtedly were duplicated elsewhere in the Southwest. In many cases, such as that of Tafolla, female-headed households were indicative of migration patterns among the males. Alberto Camarillo, in reviewing the labor history of four nineteenth-century barrios in Southern California, found that the displacement of workers from traditional occupations forced many men to seek part-time and seasonal work outside the state.[43] This did not necessarily mean, however, that while the men were at home, between harvests or jobs, that they did not expect their women to live up to patriarchal expectations. But during the male absence, the women undoubtedly had wide authority and independence in domestic, as well as nondomestic, matters.

The Mexican-American experience with matriarchy differs substantially from that of European immigrant groups. Among the Italians, the cultural traditions and social pressures within the immigrant community were powerful enough to prevent widespread male desertion of spouses. But again, differences in the economic environment seem crucial for understanding this difference. Unlike many Mexican and Mexican-American men, Italian men found jobs in industrial factories located near their homes. Virginia Yans McLaughlin reported that, in 1905, only four percent of two thousand first-generation immigrant families were female-headed. Yet, there were some similarities with the Mexican-American experience, since many Italian families were first preceded by the husband's migration to America. The proportions of female-headed households in Italy probably rose during the period of their migration. Only in America, with the family reunited, did it appear that the Italian family was more stable than that of the Mexican American.[44] The arguments that the Italian family was usually cohesive and that this was a cultural manifestation fail to take into account differences in migration and economic opportunities.[45]

Among Mexican Americans, poverty, unemployment, and social dislocation were as prominent as among Italian immigrants, yet social control over abandonment was not evident. Perhaps Mexican-American men felt more secure about leaving their spouses and children behind, assured their extended kin and friends would take care of their family while they were gone. Moreover, the Southwest was not a strange and forbidding country to them. As the decades progressed, however, more and more women who were heads of household were forced into the job market. Obviously, the kinship support system increasingly failed to meet their needs.

Female Employment and Matriarchal Families

This raises the issue of female unemployment as a way in which traditional roles expected of women changed. As can be seen in Table 3, only a very small portion of all eligible women in any given census year were employed outside the home. There was, however, a noticeable trend of more and more women entering the job market as the century progressed. A very small number found employment as nurses, owners of small shops, secretaries or clerks, and in other white-collar jobs. A larger number, but still small percentage, worked in skilled jobs as hat makers, seamstresses, and cooks. The majority of employed women, however, worked in unskilled jobs as washerwomen, laundresses, or servants.

TABLE 3

The Percentage of Employed Mexican-American Women,
Ages 20–25, in Four Southwestern Towns

	1850	1860	1870	1880
N of Sample	546	760	1129	1230
Professionals	0	.1	.1	.5
Mercantile	0	.1	.1	.4
Skilled	.4	1.4	.3	1.8
Unskilled	.9	7.0	7.0	7.8

This pattern of increasing female employment, even on a very modest scale, continued into the next century. Camarillo discovered that in Santa Barbara and San Diego in 1910, between 15 and 16 percent of all adult women worked outside the home.[46] It is impossible to determine how many women worked in part-time jobs or in seasonal ones with their families as part of the agricultural work force, but many probably followed the crops with their families.

Women were most obviously part of the casual labor pool in the markets or the public plazas. These *mercados*, a vital part of the economic and social life of the four pueblos prior to the American era, continued after 1848 to be the nucleus of the barrio culture. Many women worked as part-time *vendadoras* selling foods, handicrafts, and a variety of household wares. The Mexican markets in Los Angeles, Tucson, Santa Fe, and San Antonio soon became tourist attractions for the Americans who wanted to partake of the "exotic" life of the Mexican-American population. The "Old Towns," reminders of this era, were places where women were able to earn a few dollars to supplement their family's income. Arnoldo de León has described the *vendadoras* of San Antonio as follows: "Young, tastefully dressed *señoritas*, the so called chili-queens, served customers heaping bowls of *chili con carne* and beans, which, with a generous supply of *tortillas*, sold for ten cents in the 1880s. . . . Or on occasions *señoritas* performed the Mexican national dances like the Hat Dance."[47] Some Mexican-American families of that city even converted their homes into restaurants to capitalize on American interest in Mexican cuisine. Their homes became showplaces for women's domestic talents.

The number of women who worked full-time in occupations was surprisingly low, given the increasingly dire economic straits of most families. This was probably because there were only a limited number of opportunities for service-type jobs as laundresses, seamstresses and the like. Industrial jobs were few and not open to many women, and commercial shops probably had bars against the employment of too many Mexican girls. Moreover, female employment was not really very pronounced, even among European immigrants in eastern cities where there were many more opportunities for full-time jobs. Thomas Kesner, for example, found that in New York in the late nineteenth century, only 2 percent of the Jewish immigrant wives and only 6 percent of married Italian women had paying jobs. In Buffalo, New York, near the turn of the century, about 25 percent of the Polish wives worked outside the home. This was the highest percentage recorded for married women; for other immigrant groups it was much lower. Reviewing this evidence, which seems to contradict the common notion that large numbers of immigrant women were forced into menial jobs, Carl Degler concluded that "at no time did more than 10 or 15 percent of wives of any immigrant nationality work outside the home, and usually the proportion was even smaller than that. . . . the propensity of wives to work outside the home is largely an ethnic, rather than a class, phenomenon."[48]

Among Italian immigrants as among Mexican Americans, there were strong prejudices against married women working in jobs which would take them away from their household obligations, give them financial independence, and cast doubt on their husband's ability to support a family. Mario García, who studied the Mexican immigrants of El Paso during the period 1880 to 1920, found that among married immigrant women "no mothers, and almost no daughters, most being too young, worked outside the home."[49] The same was true for the urban Mexican-American population in other towns of the Southwest before the turn of the century. There were, however, some important exceptions.

Table 4 presents clear evidence of the effect that the economy had on family structure. Women with children but no husband were progressively forced to enter the job market because they lacked a wage-earning spouse, or because relatives were unable to provide entirely for their needs. These women were more likely to be employed than either married women with spouses present or single women without families. Surprisingly fewer and fewer women who lived as relatives within extended families became job holders as the decades progressed. This indicated that the formation of extended families was not entirely related to economic pressures. Female employment was a strategy for the survival of matriarchal, not nuclear or extended, families.

The reality of women working and being heads of families was bound to challenge the traditional male expectations regarding patriarchy.

TABLE 4

The Household Status of Employed Mexican-American Women, Ages 16–59

	1850	1860	1870	1880
N of Sample	7	66	61	129
Head of HH	28.6	43.9	47.5	39.5
Spouse	14.3	7.5	14.8	3.1
Child (under 21)	14.3	15.1	14.8	23.3
Relative	14.3	10.6	3.3	3.1
Unrelated Adult	14.3	22.7	19.7	24.8

But then it would be wrong to assume that all women were equally affected by these changes. The overwhelming majority of women were not, and the upper classes hardly at all. The small but significant Mexican-American middle and professional class did not experience many broken families and, of course, they were the ones to whom patriarchal ideals were most sacrosanct.

Patriarchal values did not disappear under the impact of economic and political changes in the urban Southwest. Men continued to expect their women to be submissive and their daughters to remain cloistered in the home. But in this respect, they were not much different from the majority of American men, who had their own kind of patriarchal ideology, sometimes described as the "Cult of True Womanhood." This image of the ideal woman, expressed in the popular and religious literature of the nineteenth century, held that "True Women" had four attributes: "piety, purity, submissiveness, and domesticity." Women were held hostage in the home to all the virtues which men held in high esteem but neglected in everyday life.[50]

The idealization of the domestic woman has been seen as one of the main characteristics of the emerging middle-class American family.[51] In this regard, the Mexican and Latin American families had been "modern" for hundreds of years. For them, family life increasingly became a mixture of the old and the new values regarding paternal authority and the proper sphere for women. Increasingly poverty and economic insecurity intensified the pressures on Mexican-American nuclear families and led to increased matriarchy and working single mothers. As a result, the ideology of patriarchy found less confirmation in everyday life. As a system of values and beliefs, however, it continued to exist.

About the Contributors

Christon I. Archer is Professor and Chair of the Department of History at the University of Calgary. He is the author of *The Bourbon Army in Mexico, 1760-1810* (Albuquerque: University of New Mexico Press, 1977), which won the Bolton Prize. He has published numerous articles on the military during the Independence Movement.

Patricia Galeana de Valadés is the Director of the Dirección General de Intercambio Académico of the Universidad Nacional Autónoma de México. She has published various articles on liberalism and the Reform.

María del Refugio González is the Director of the Centro de Estudios Sobre la Universidad of the Universidad Nacional Autónoma de México. She is the author of *Historia del Derecho mexicano* (México: Universidad Nacional Autónoma de México, 1981). She has published widely on legal history, particularly during the nineteenth century. She is completing a study of conservative thought in the early nineteenth century.

Richard Griswold del Castillo is Professor of Mexican American Studies at San Diego State University. He is the author of *The Los Angeles Barrio, 1850-1890: A Social History* (Berkeley: University of California Press, 1979) and *La Familia: Chicano Families in the Urban Southwest 1848 to the Present* (Notre Dame: Notre Dame University Press, 1984).

Jaime E. Rodríguez O. is Professor of History and Director of the Mexico/Chicano Program at the University of California, Irvine. He is the author of *The Emergence of Spanish America: Vicente Rocafuerte and Spanish Americanism, 1808-1832* (Berkeley: University of California

Press, 1975) and with Colin M. MacLachlan, *The Forging of the Cosmic Race: A Reinterpretation of Colonial Mexico* (Berkeley: University of California Press, 1980).

Barbara A. Tenenbaum is a historian who lives in Washington, D.C. She is the author of *The Politics of Penury: Debts and Taxes in Mexico, 1821–1856* (Albuquerque: University of New Mexico Press, 1986). She is currently engaged in a study of the effects of the Treaty of Guadalupe Hidalgo.

Notes

1 Down from Colonialism: Mexico's Nineteenth-Century Crisis

* This essay is an expanded and revised version of my Distinguished Faculty Lecture. It is published here with permission of the Regents of the University of California.
[1] This discussion is based on my work with Colin M. MacLachlan, *The Forging of the Cosmic Race: A Reinterpretation of Colonial Mexico* (Berkeley: U of California P, 1980).
[2] Henry G. Ward, *Mexico in 1827,* 2nd ed., 2 vols. (London, 1829) 1: 383.
[3] David Brading has written extensively on mining. See: *Miners and Merchants in Bourbon Mexico, 1780-1810* (Cambridge: Cambridge UP, 1971); "La minería de la plata en el siglo XVIII: el caso de Bolanos," *Historia mexicana* 18 (1969): 317-33; "Mexican Silver in the 18th Century: The Revival of Zacatecas," *Hispanic American Historical Review* 53 (1973): 389-414. See also Roberto Moreno, "Las instituciones de la industria minera novohispana," in Miguel León Portilla et al., *La minería en México* (México: Universidad Nacional Autónoma de México, 1978) 68-164.
[4] John H. Coatsworth, "Obstacles to Economic Growth in Nineteenth-Century Mexico," *American Historical Review* 83.1 (1978): 82.
[5] There have been several attempts to calculate both the GNP and the per capita income of Mexico ca. 1800 from the data gathered by José María Quirós, *Memoria de estatuto* (Veracruz, 1817). See, for example, Fernando Rosenzweig Hernández, "La economía novo-hispana al comenzar el siglo XIX," *Ciencias políticas y sociales* 9 (1963): 455-94; Doris M. Ladd, *The Mexican Nobility at Independence* (Austin: Institute of Latin American Studies, U of Texas, 1976) 26. Henry G. Aubrey, "The National Income of Mexico," *I.A.S.I. Estadística* (June 1950): 185-98, based his conclusion on Alexander von Humboldt, *Essai politique sur le royaume de la Nouvelle-Espagne,* 5 vols. (Paris, 1811). Clark W. Reynolds compared Aubrey's and Rosenzweig's figures in "The Per Capita Income of New Spain Before Independence and After the Revolution," *The Mexican Economy* (New Haven: Yale UP, 1970). John H. Coatsworth has recently re-examined New Spain's per capita income in his "Obstacles to Eco-

nomic Growth." Unfortunately, he neither lists his sources for Mexico clearly nor does he explain his method.

Aside from minor errors of computation found in the figures originally published by Humboldt and Quirós, the major problem in calculating GNP in 1800 is establishing the correct size of New Spain's population. Most scholars generally accept 6 million as the size of Mexico's population ca. 1810. There are two problems with that figure. If one accepts the number, the subsequent population growth in the next four decades is so low as to be nonexistent. Such a phenomenon is not consistent with the facts. Also, the census of 1793 arrives at a much lower figure. That census, which was the only serious count obtained in the period under consideration, has always had its critics. Contemporaries, like José de Alzate, Alexander von Humboldt, Fernando Navarro y Noriega, Juan López Cancelada, and Tadeo Ortiz de Ayala, subjected the enumeration to criticism and raised the count substantially. Recently, critics have reviewed the census and given their own assessments; see, for example, Victoria Lerner, "La población de la Nueva España," *Historia mexicana* 28 (1968): 327-46; Romeo Flores Caballero, *La contrarrevolución en la independencia* (México: Colegio de México, 1969) 15-24; and Gonzalo Aguirre Beltrán, *La población negra de México,* 2nd ed. (México: Fondo de Cultura Económica, 1972) 230 and passim. I find Aguirre Beltrán's analysis the most searching and, in my view, the most nearly accurate. He concludes that the population of New Spain, exclusive of Cuba, Central America, and the Philippines, was approximately 3,799,561. Therefore, I have used 4,000,000 as the population of New Spain in 1800. Although this, in effect, raised my estimated per capita income, I am convinced it represents a sound estimate.

In comparing Mexican with United States and English per capita incomes, I have relied on Coatsworth where his figures do not conflict with mine, because he has the best data for the other countries and for later periods of Mexican history. I have followed him in using 1950 dollars as a basis of comparison for per capita income calculations. But I have retained the original figures for GNP in 1800 to allow a direct comparison with the calculations made by Quirós and his contemporaries.

[6] Aguirre Beltrán, *La población negra* 230.

[7] MacLachlan and Rodríguez, *The Forging of the Cosmic Race* 196-228.

[8] The political history of postindependence Mexico remains confused. Among the best studies are: William S. Robertson, *Iturbide of Mexico* (Durham: Duke UP, 1952); Flores Caballero, *La contrarrevolución;* Jaime E. Rodríguez O., *The Emergence of Spanish America* (Berkeley: U of California P, 1975); Michael P. Costeloe, *La primera República Federal de México 1824-1835* (México: Fondo de Cultura Económica, 1975); Charles Macune, *El Estado de México y la federación mexicana* (México: Fondo de Cultura Económica, 1978); Fernando Díaz Díaz, *Caudillos y caciques* (México: El Colegio de México, 1972); Moisés González Navarro, *Anatomía del poder en México* (México: El Colegio de México, 1977).

[9] Karl Marx in Karl Marx and Friedrich Engels, *Collected Works,* 16 vols. (New York: International Publishers, 1976) 8: 365-66. Marx also acknowledged that Mexicans in the conquered territories would lose their "independence" and suffer from discrimination but, in his view, that did not matter in comparison to the progress which the Americans would bring. Similarly,

Engels declared: "In America we have witnessed the conquest of Mexico and have rejoiced at it . . . It is to the interest of its own development that Mexico will be placed under the tutelage of the United States." Marx and Engels, *Collected Works* 6: 527. Although both men justified their views on the grounds that the United States was bringing capitalism to a feudal Mexico, it is clear that racist beliefs colored their analysis. In their works, Mexicans are described as "lazy," "decadent," and "degenerate," while Americans are called "energetic," "dynamic," and "progressive."

[10] Jenaro González Reyna, *Riqueza minera y yacimientos minerales de México* (México: Banco de México, 1947) 109.

[11] Miguel Lerdo de Tejada, *El comercio exterior de México*, 2nd ed. (México: Banco Nacional de Comercio Exterior, 1976), unnumbered tables; Inés Herrera Canales, *El comercio exterior de México, 1821-1875* (México: El Colegio de México, 1977) 58-75.

[12] Coatsworth, "Obstacles to Economic Growth" 82 and passim.

[13] The contraction in commerce can be seen, for example, in the reduced activities of entrepreneurs such as the Sánchez Navarros; Charles H. Harris, *A Mexican Family Empire: The Latifundio of the Sánchez-Navarro Family, 1765-1867* (Austin: U of Texas P, 1975); Díaz Díaz, *Caudillos y caciques* examines the role of regional bosses; and Harry Cross looks at "Living Standards in Rural Nineteenth-Century Mexico: Zacatecas, 1820-1880," *Journal of Latin American Studies* 10.1 (1978): 1-19.

[14] The best work on Mexican geography is Jorge L. Tamayo, *Geografía general de México*, 4 vols., 2nd ed. (México: Instituto Mexicano de Investigaciones Económicas, 1962). See also, Claude Bataillon, *Las regiones geográficas en México* (México: Siglo XXI, 1969).

[15] On the problems of land transportation, see: Salvador Ortiz Valadés, *La arriería en México* (México: n.p., 1929) and Peter Rees, *Transportes y comercio entre México y Veracruz, 1519-1910* (México: Secretaría de Educación Pública, 1976). David R. Ringrose presents an excellent analysis of similar problems in the mother country in *Transportation and Economic Stagnation in Spain, 1750-1850* (Durham: Duke UP, 1970).

[16] Flores Caballero, *La contrarrevolución* 66-82. Christon Archer argues, in "The Royalist Army in New Spain: Civil-Military Relationships, 1810-1821" *Journal of Latin American Studies* 13.1 (1981): 79-80, that armed groups controlled most of the country during the wars of independence. In his view, the national government had lost all control in the provinces.

[17] Hugh M. Hamill, Jr. discusses Mora's estimates in "Was the Mexican Independence Movement a Revolution?" *Dos revoluciones: México y los Estados Unidos* (México: Banamex, 1976) 43-61.

[18] Joel R. Poinsett, *Notes on Mexico* (Philadelphia, 1824) 178-79.

[19] G. F. Lyon, *Journal of a Residence and Tour in the Republic of Mexico in 1826*, 2 vols. (London, 1828) 1: 192-93.

[20] Lucas Alamán, *Historia de Méjico*, 5 vols. (México, 1942) 2: 65-66.

[21] Quoted in Ladd, *The Mexican Nobility* 147.

[22] For an excellent description of *léperos*, see Poinsett, *Notes on Mexico*, and Fanny Calderón de la Barca, *Life in Mexico* (New York: Doubleday, 1966) 91-92.

[23] Ward, *Mexico* 1: 298-400.

[24] Ibid.; Quirós, *Memoria de estatuto* 24-29.
[25] On British mining investments, see Newton R. Gilmore, "British Mining Ventures in Early National Mexico," diss., U of California, Berkeley, 1956, and Robert W. Randall, *Real del Monte: A British Mining Venture in Mexico* (Austin: U of Texas P, 1972).
[26] Robert A. Potash, *El Banco de Avío de México: el fomento de la industria, 1821-1846* (Mexico: Fondo de Cultura Económica, 1959); Dawn Keremitsis, *La industria textil mexicana en el siglo XIX* (México: Secretaría de Educación Pública, 1973).
[27] Ladd, *The Mexican Nobility* 139-40. On small farmers, see David Brading, *Haciendas and Ranchos in the Mexican Bajío: León, 1700-1860* (Cambridge: Cambridge UP, 1978).
[28] The study of nineteenth-century Mexican agriculture remains in its infancy. Among the best works are: Brading, *Haciendas and Ranchos;* Eric van Young, "Rural Life in Eighteenth-Century Mexico: The Guadalajara Region, 1675-1820," diss., U of California, Berkeley, 1978; the works of Jan Bazant, among them, *Cinco haciendas mexicanas* (México: El Colegio de México, 1975); and Harris, *A Mexican Family Empire.* Although not limited to agriculture, Harry E. Cross, "The Mining Economy of Zacatecas, Mexico in the Nineteenth Century," diss., U of California, Berkeley, 1976, provides much information on rural conditions.
[29] Lerdo de Tejada, *El comercio exterior;* Herrera Canales, *El comercio exterior* 58-71; González Reyna, *Riqueza minera* 109-10.
[30] The best study of the Church as a banker is Michael P. Costeloe, *Church Wealth in Mexico* (Cambridge: Cambridge UP, 1976). Richard Lindley discusses the nature of personal credit and its decline in "Kinship and Credit in the Structure of Guadalajara's Oligarchy, 1800-1830," diss., U of Texas, Austin, 1975.
[31] MacLachlan and Rodríguez, *The Forging of the Cosmic Race* 262-99.
[32] Flores Caballero, *La contrarrevolución* 28-65; Asunción Lavrin, "The Execution of the Law of Consolidation in New Spain," *Hispanic American Historical Review* 52 (1973): 27-49.
[33] Humboldt, *Essai politique.*

2 Where Did All the Royalists Go? New Light on the Military Collapse of New Spain, 1810-1822

[1] Félix Calleja to Francisco Xavier de Venegas, Guanajuato, August 14, 1811, Archivo General de la Nación, México (cited hereinafter as AGN), Ramo de Operaciones de Guerra (cited hereinafter as OG), vol. 190; and José de la Cruz to Venegas, December 31, 1810, AGN:OG, vol. 142.
[2] Calleja to Venegas, Zitaquaro, August 11, 1811, AGN:OG, vol. 190.
[3] Conde de la Cadena to Venegas, Villa de Lagos, January 7, 1811, AGN:OG, vol. 94-A.
[4] See for example, Petition of Celaya residents led by José Antonio Lanona, February 9, 1811, AGN:OG, vol. 30.

NOTES TO CHAPTER 2

[5] Manuel de Acevedo, Intendente de San Luis Potosí, to Calleja, San Luis Potosí, October 17, 1810, AGN:OG, vol. 91; Correspondence of Calleja, 1810–1811, AGN:OG, vol. 180; and Francisco Rendón to Venegas, January 27, 1811, AGN:OG, vol. 171.
[6] José de la Cruz to Calleja, September 10, 1814, AGN:OG, vol. 161.
[7] José Alonso Terán to Conde de la Cadena, October 3, 1810, AGN:OG, vol 94-A. Also see Lucas Alamán, *Historia de Méjico* (México: Editorial Jus, 1968) 1:247. On the approach to the town of Celaya, Hidalgo threatened to execute 78 European prisoners.
[8] Venegas to Calleja, December 8, 1810, AGN:OG, vol. 170.
[9] Cruz to Venegas, November 30, 1810, AGN:OG, vol. 141. The royalist forces burned the town to the ground and executed any suspicious males found without passports in the district. Their bodies were hung up as graphic object lessons.
[10] Cruz to Venegas, Valladolid, December 28, 1810, AGN:OG, vol. 142. Cruz freed 170 Europeans who were in the prisons of Valladolid when he occupied the city. Also see Hugh M. Hamill, *The Hidalgo Revolt: Prelude to Mexican Independence* (Gainesville: U of Florida P, 1966) 183.
[11] Calleja to the Minister of War, March 15, 1813, Archivo General de Indias (cited hereinafter as AGI), Mexico, leg. 1322; Carlos María Bustamante, *Cuadro histórico de la Revolución de Independencia* (México: Cámara de Diputados, 1961) 1:133–34; and Hugh M. Hamill, "Royalist Counterinsurgency in the Mexican War of Independence: The Lessons of 1811," *HAHR* 53 (1973): 486.
[12] Calleja to Venegas, August 12, 1811, AGN:OG, vol. 190.
[13] Calleja to Venegas, Guadalajara, January 18 and 29, 1811, AGN:OG, vol. 171. For a good example of the difficulties see Correspondence of Sub-Inspector Carlos de Urrutía, AGN:OG, vol. 882, 1810–1812. At Veracruz, Urrutía attempted to enlist a militia force of 1,000 merchants and members of the *gente decente* classes. The port city elite refused to accept military discipline. See José María de Almansa, commander of the Regimiento de Voluntarios Distinguidos de Fernando VII de Veracruz, to Venegas, January 24, 1812, AGN:OG, vol. 882.
[14] Romeo Flores Caballero, *La contrarrevolución en la independencia: Los españoles en la vida política, social y económica de México (1804–1838)* (México: Colegio de México, 1969) 69; and Venegas to Calleja, February 3, 1811, AGN:OG, vol. 181.
[15] Bando sobre alistamiento general, October 26, 1813, Article 6, AGI, Mexico, leg. 1146; and Timothy E. Anna, *The Fall of the Royal Government in Mexico City* (Lincoln: U of Nebraska P, 1978) 127.
[16] Report of the Council of Indies, May 25, 1816, AGI, Mexico, leg. 1146.
[17] Bando of Calleja, February 9, 1815, AGI, Mexico, leg. 1146.
[18] Ibid.
[19] Report of the Council of Indies, May 25, 1816, AGI, Mexico, leg. 1146.
[20] Memo of the Regency, Cádiz, 1811, AGI, Mexico, leg. 1321.
[21] Marqués de Campo Sagrado to the Secretario de Hacienda, Palacio, September 10, 1816, AGI, Mexico, leg. 2430.
[22] Cabildo of Jalapa to Venegas, October 5, 1812, AGN:OG, vol. 32.
[23] Cabildo of Jalapa to Calleja, April 27, 1813, AGN:OG, vol. 32; and

Colonel Juan María Soto, Gobernador Interino de Veracruz, to the Minister of War, no. 34, November 21, 1812, Archivo Militar de Segovia, Segovia, Spain (cited hereinafter as AMS), Ultramar, leg. 230. The Infantry Battalion of Fernando VII was blockaded in Veracruz by insurgent attacks.

[24] Melchor Alvarez to Calleja, July 13, 1813, and Calleja to Alvarez, August 4, 1813, AGN:OG, vol. 1.

[25] Christon I. Archer, "The Royalist Army in New Spain: Civil-Military Relationships," *Journal of Latin American Studies* 13 (1981): 79–80; and Lucas Alamán, *Historia de Méjico* 4: 312.

[26] José María Echeagaray to Juan Busmao Bestard, San Juan de Ulúa, August 2, 1817, AMS, Ultramar, leg. 223.

[27] *Ibid.*, and Report of the Secretario de la Cámara, Madrid, February 28, 1820, AMS, Ultramar, leg. 223. Echeagaray was 56 years of age at this time and he possessed sufficient experience to hold senior offices. His biological resistance to yellow fever because of his birth at the port city made him an excellent potential candidate. Despite his merits, the regime continued to place unacclimatized but better connected officers into the deathtrap of Veracruz. In conversations with former creole royalist officers, Lucas Alamán encountered the same attitudes expressed by Echeagaray. See Lucas Alamán, *Historia de Méjico* 5:35.

[28] Cabildo of Mexico to Calleja, October 20, 1815, AGN:OG, vol. 32. The viceroy responded by republishing a Bando of October 24, 1813, outlining penalties for these crimes. For example, a soldier received punishment of one month in irons for stealing fruit or refusing to pay just prices. Each unit of the garrison was to send sergeants into the markets from 7:00 to 9:00 a.m. to police their soldiers while they purchased their daily food. Obviously, the Bando had limited impact.

[29] Petition of the Ayuntamiento of Izucar and letters by residents, August 16, 1820, AGN:OG, vol. 325.

[30] Pascual de Liñan to Apodaca, no. 1561, October 27, 1818, AGN:OG, vol. 501.

[31] Mariano Gil, Comandante Militar of Puente del Rey to the Comandante Interino del Camino Militar, Lieutenant Colonel José María Travesi, June 11, 1819, AGN:OG, vol. 496.

[32] Ciriaco de Llano to Venadito, reservado, October 12, 1820, AGN:OG, vol. 461.

[33] Llano to Venadito, no. 1141, December 20, 1820, AGN:OG, vol. 461.

[34] Juan Rafols to Venadito, Cutzamala, June 16, 1819, AGN:OG, vol. 814.

[35] Rafols to Venadito, August 12, 1820, AGN:OG, vol. 814.

[36] Liñan to Apodaca, no. 1032, August 6, 1818, AGN:OG, vol. 499; and Liñan to Apodaca, no. 568, May 22, 1818, AGN:OG, vol. 491.

[37] Liñan to Apodaca, no. 1052, August 9, 1818, AGN:OG, vol. 499.

[38] In 1816, the first battalion was garrisoned in Mexico City while the second battalion went to the healthy Llanos de Apam, where the climate was good and provisions were plentiful. Later, the second battalion served in the difficult campaign against the Javier de Mina invasion, and following the sieges it was garrisoned at Guanajuato. Three companies left at Apam were sent to the Camino Militar de Jalapa to pursue the guerrillas of Guadalupe Vic-

NOTES TO CHAPTER 2 109

toria. These units suffered severely from yellow fever and the harsh conditions caused by the climate.
[39] Apodaca to Liñan, September 1, 1818, AGN:OG, vol. 488.
[40] Ibid.
[41] Ibid.
[42] A Royal Order of September 30, 1819, promised 3,000 Spanish recruits for the expeditionary battalions. Liñan spent considerable time devising schemes to divide the incoming replacements among the expeditionary units stationed in Mexico. Events in Spain, culminating with the Riego Rebellion, prevented the dispatch of any replacements. See Liñan to Venadito, no. 353, March 11, 1820, AGN:OG, vol. 502. For the imperial side of the replacement question, see Xavier Castaños to Miguel de Ladizábal, Madrid, October 12, 1814, AMS, Ultramar, leg. 226; and José de Ymar to the Secretario de Hacienda de Indias, Palacio, October 5, 1819, AGI, Mexico, leg. 2420.
[43] Despite Apodaca's appeals for replacements, the question was not dealt with in Madrid until well into 1819.
[44] Antonio Linares, Comandante General de Guanajuato, to Venadito, Celaya, August 1, 1820, AGN:OG, vol. 460.
[45] Linares to Venadito, no. 295, September 1, 1820, AGN:OG, vol. 460.
[46] Ayuntamiento of Miacatlán to the Presidente y Vocales de la Exma. Diputación Provincial de México, November 4, 1820, AGN:OG, vol. 455.
[47] Llano to Venadito, no. 1850, September 11, 1820, AGN:OG, vol. 461.
[48] Llano to Venadito, no. 1292, March 28, 1821, AGN:OG, vol. 326.
[49] José García Figueroa to Ramón Gutiérrez de Mazo, Intendente de México, Sinacatepec, July 10, 1820, AGN:OG, vol. 391.
[50] José María Torres to Venadito, Santa Ana de México, November 23, 1820, AGN:OG, vol. 457.
[51] Francisco de Ortiz, Primer Alcalde de Huejutla to Gutiérrez de Mazo, January 22, 1821, AGN:OG, vol. 455.
[52] Rafols to Venadito, August 12, 1820, AGN:OG, vol. 814.
[53] Liñan to Venadito, no. 82, Veracruz, March 3, 1819, AGN:OG, vol. 490.
[54] Antonio López de Santa Ana to Venadito, Mexico, December 4, 1818, AGN:OG, vol. 490.
[55] Liñan to Venadito, no. 1089, July 27, 1810; and Instancia de Iturbide, n.d., 1820, AGN:OG, vol. 502.
[56] Llano to Venadito, no. 1246, March 13, 1821, AGN:OG, vol. 326. For similar events in Puebla, see Llano to Venadito, no. 1222, March 4, 1821, AGN:OG, vol. 326.
[57] See Brian R. Hamnett, "Anastasio Bustamante y la guerra de independencia, 1810–1821," *Historia Mexicana* 28 (1979): 515–45.
[58] Manuel Merino to Venadito, Valladolid, April 4, 1821, AGN:OG, vol. 779.
[59] Llano to Venadito, no. 1225, March 6, 1821, AGN:OG, vol. 326.
[60] Llano to Venadito, no. 1339, April 12, 1821, AGN:OG, vol. 327.
[61] Llano to Venadito, no. 222, March 4, 1821, AGN:OG, vol. 326.
[62] Linares to Venadito, nos. 58 and 59, March 25 and 26, 1821, AGN:OG, vol. 460

[63] Venadito to Linares, March 29, 1821, AGN:OG, vol. 460. The viceroy ordered Linares to report to Querétaro, where he would have to justify his conduct. Petitions from Linares's supporters defended his actions and pointed out that no commander could have resisted the popular revolt.

[64] Rafols to Venadito, Lerma, March 8, 1821, AGN:OG, vol. 814.

[65] Correspondence of José Joaquín Márquez y Donallo, April and May 1821, AGN:OG, vol. 779. For information on Hevia, see Ayudante Mayor Domingo Travieso to Tomás Barrera, Brigadier de la Armada Nacional, Cádiz, December 10, 1821, AGI, Indiferente General, leg. 1569.

[66] Liñan to Venadito, no. 604, May 12, 1821, AGN:OG, vol. 501.

[67] Llano to Venadito, nos. 1388 and 1384, April 29, 1821, AGN:OG, vol. 327.

[68] See Timothy E. Anna, "Francisco Novella and the Last Stand of the Royal Army in New Spain," *HAHR* 51 (1971): 92-111.

[69] Apodaca to the Minister of War, June 21, 1821, AMS, Ultramar, leg. 227.

[70] Report of the Consejo de la Guerra, September 1, 1821, AMS, Ultramar, leg. 227.

[71] José de la Cruz to Venadito, March 9, 1821, AGN:OG, vol. 148. Also see E. Christiansen, *The Origins of Military Power in Spain, 1800-1854* (Oxford: Oxford UP, 1967) 22.

[72] Luaces to José Dávila, February 22, 1822, AMS, Ultramar, leg. 227.

[73] Apodaca to the Secretario del Estado y del Despacho de la Guerra, Guanabacoa, Cuba, November 17, 1821, AMS, Ultramar, leg. 224. For details on the bleak future for the Spaniards, see Harold D. Sims, *La expulsión de los españoles de México, 1821-1828* (México: Fondo de Cultura Económica, 1974); and *Descolonización en México. El conflicto entre mexicanos y españoles, 1821-1831* (México: Fondo de Cultura Económica, 1982).

[74] Llano to the Ministro de Estado y del Despacho de la Guerra, Havana, January 30, 1822, AMS, Ultramar, leg. 228.

3 Los liberales y la Iglesia

[1] cf. Oscar Handling, *La verdad en la Historia* (México: Fondo de Cultura Económica, 1982) 90 y ss.

[2] cf. Abelardo Villegas, *México en el horizonte liberal* (México: Universidad Nacional Autónoma de México, 1981).

[3] Ives M. Congar, *Sacerdocio y laicado* (Madrid: Ed. Estela, 1964) 47.

[4] Otto Hintze, *Historia de las formas políticas* (Madrid: Ediciones de la Revista de Occidente, 1976) 81 y ss.

[5] García Icazbaldeta en Carlos Pereyra, *Historia de la América Española* (Madrid: Ed. Saturnino Calleja, 1924).

[6] Francisco López Cámara, *La estructura económica y social de México en la época de la Reforma* (México: Siglo XXI, 1967) 29, 196 y ss.

[7] Robert Ricard, *La conquista espiritual de México* (México: Ed. Jus, 1974) 424.

[8] Jean Touchard, *Historia de las ideas políticas* (Madrid: Ed. Tecnos, 1969) 401-02.

[9] Roberto Moreno y de los Arcos, "La última Nueva España", *La formación del Estado mexicano,* ed. María del Refugio González (México: Ed. Porrúa, 1984) 15-29.
[10] Rodolfo Pastor, "De la autonomía ilustrada a la Revolución", *México y su Historia* (México: Ed. Uthea, 1984) 4: 111-63.
[11] Charles Hale, *El liberalismo en México de la época de Mora* (México: Siglo XXI, 1978) 304-09.
[12] Edmundo O'Gorman, *México: el trauma de su historia* (México: Universidad Nacional Autónoma de México, 1977) 23 y ss.
[13] José María Luis Mora, *Obras sueltas* (París: Librería de la Rosa, 1837) 1: 92-93. No obstante su anticlericalismo y las simpatías protestantes que también le han atribuido, en su proyecto del partido liberal en materia de cultos, declara que la tolerancia podía y debía "diferirse indefinidamente en razón de que no habiendo mexicanos que profesen otro culto que el católico romano", tampoco había, como en otros países, "la necesidad de garantizarlos" y se limita a pedir la libertad de opiniones escritas, o libertad de prensa.
[14] Martín Quirarte, *El problema religioso en México* (México: Instituto Nacional de Antropología e Historia, 1967) 167 y ss.
[15] La Ley Lerdo fue duramente criticada por Melchor Ocampo en un extenso memorial que dirigió al Presidente Juárez el 22 de octubre de 1859, para "que quede en los archivos". Allí Ocampo acusó a Lerdo de haber reconocido en favor del clero una propiedad que nunca tuvo. Véase Jorge L. Tamayo, *Benito Juárez. Documentos, discursos y correspondencia* (México: Ed. Libros de México, 1972) 4: 234 y ss.
[16] Protesta del Arzobispo Pelagio Antonio Labastida y Dávalos por la política eclesiástica que querían imponer los franceses. La protesta formal del Arzobispo se publicó en el *Diario Oficial,* así como en *L'Estafette* del 25 de octubre de 1863.
[17] En *Apuntes para mis hijos,* Juárez no formula opinión alguna que pueda considerarse crítica para el credo católico; sí lo hace, empero, con relación al clero mismo. En la vida política de Juárez podemos encontrar igual su concurrencia a un Te Deum, que su rúbrica precedida por un "Dios y Libertad". Sin embargo, su pensamiento político fue orientándose progresivamente en el sentido de que la función política y la vocación religiosa, si bien compatibles en una misma persona, demandaban un ejercicio diferenciado. "Los gobernantes de la sociedad civil no deben asistir como tales a ninguna ceremonia eclesiástica, si bien como hombres pueden ir a los templos a practicar los actos de devoción que su religión les dicte". Véase Tamayo 4: 271.
[18] Guy Palmade, "La época de la burguesía", *Historia Universal* (Madrid: Siglo XXI, 1976) 248. Max Weber, *Economía y sociedad* (México: Fondo de Cultura Económica, 1944) 2: 244.
[19] Jesús Reyes Heroles, *El liberalismo mexicano* (México: Fondo de Cultura Económica, 1974) 3: 244.
[20] Georges Bourdeau, *Le Liberalisme* (París: Editions Du Seuil, 1979) 131 y ss.
[21] cf. José C. Valadés, *El pensamiento político de Benito Juárez* (México: Librería de Manuel Porrúa, 1972) 141 y ss.

4 El pensamiento de los conservadores mexicanos

[1] Edmund Burke, *Reflections on the Revolution in France and the Proceedings in certain Societies in London relative to that Event,* ed. Conor Cruise O'Brien (Great Britain: Pelican Classics, 1969).

[2] "Macropedia", *Enciclopedia Británica* 1974.

[3] Burke mismo caería en el supuesto, ya que estudios recientes revelan su filiación católica y su rechazo a la política inglesa frente a Irlanda.

[4] Sobre este tema existe la obra de Alfonso Noriega, *El pensamiento conservador y el conservadurismo mexicano,* 2 vols. (México: Universidad Nacional Autónoma de México, 1972).

[5] A propósito eludo el uso del vocablo "soberanía" porque su alcance es objeto de diversas interpretaciones.

[6] Ver Felipe Tena Ramírez, *Leyes fundamentales de México (1808-1975),* 6a. ed. (México: Porrúa, 1975). Por otra parte, la bibliografía sobre los justos títulos de España sobre las Indias es amplísima. Una selección puede consultarse en la obra citada en Nota 8.

[7] Roberto Moreno, "La última Nueva España", *La formación del Estado mexicano,* ed. María del Refugio González (México: Ed. Porrúa, 1984) 15-29.

[8] María del Refugio González, *Historia del derecho mexicano* (México: Universidad Nacional Autónoma de México, 1981). Aunque no está actualizada, hay una orientación bibliográfica de alguna utilidad sobre estos temas en el apartado VIII.

[9] González 3.

[10] Ver la introducción de Cruise O'Brien en Burke.

[11] Clemente de Jesús Munguía, *Del Derecho Natural en sus principios comunes y en sus diversas ramificaciones, o sea, Curso elemental de Derecho Natural y de gentes, público, político, constitucional y principios de legislación,* 3 vols. (México: Imprenta de la Voz de la Religión, 1849).

[12] Enrique Denzinger, *El magisterio de la Iglesia* (Barcelona: Herder, 1963). En toda la parte relativa a los Papas desde 1600 a 1780, y entre 1800 y 1878.

5 "Neither a borrower nor a lender be": Financial Constraints and the Treaty of Guadalupe Hidalgo

The idea for this paper came out of a series of conversations between the author and Mr. Raúl Yzaguirre, President, National Council of La Raza, Washington, D.C. The author would also like to thank Dr. Guadalupe Jiménez Codinach, Professor of History, Universidad Ibero-Americana, Mexico City, and Dr. John Hébert, Assistant Chief, Hispanic Division, Library of Congress, for their helpful comments.

[1] The remainder of the southwestern boundary line was completed with the Gadsden Purchase (Treaty of La Mesilla) in 1854.

[2] These claims totaled $3,250,000. It should be noted that at this time the Mexican peso was exactly equivalent to the United States' dollar and that "$" was commonly used for both currencies.

NOTES TO CHAPTER 5

[3] These figures were generated by comparing categories used in Mexico City and Veracruz in 1760 and 1790 as shown in John J. TePaske with the collaboration of José and Mari Luz Hernández Palomo, *La Real Hacienda de Nueva España: La real caja de México (1576-1816)* (México: Departamento de Investigaciones Históricas, 1976).

[4] This conclusion has been confirmed by TePaske.

[5] Doris Ladd, *The Mexican Nobility at Independence* (Austin: Institute of Latin American Studies, U of Texas, 1976) 99, 100-103.

[6] Brian R. Hamnett, *Revolución y contrarrevolución en México y el Perú. Liberalismo, realeza y separatismo 1800-1824* (México: Fondo de Cultura Económica, 1978) 81-88, 152-53.

[7] Ladd 148-53; Charles W. Macune, Jr., *El estado de México y la federación mexicana 1823-1835* (México: Fondo de Cultura Económica, 1978) 67, 72- 79.

[8] Jaime E. Rodríguez O., *The Emergence of Spanish America. Vicente Rocafuerte and Spanish Americanism 1808-1832* (Berkeley: U of California P, 1975) 111, 116-18.

[9] Miguel Lerdo de Tejada, *Comercio exterior de México desde la Conquista hasta hoy* (México: Banco Nacional de Comercio Exterior, 1967) chart 43.

[10] Rodríguez O. 120-24, 127.

[11] *Memoria de Hacienda 1870* (México, 1870) 68-71; *El Sol* 28 November 1827, 3690-91, and *El Sol* 29 November 1827, 3693, as cited in Romeo Flores Caballero, *Counterrevolution, The Role of the Spaniards in the Independence of Mexico, 1804-1838*, trans. Jaime Rodríguez O. (Lincoln: U of Nebraska P, 1974) 103.

[12] Flores Caballero 129.

[13] *Memoria de Hacienda 1870* 96.

[14] *Memoria de Hacienda 1844*, chart 7 for the figures on internal loans. These should be considered as indicative rather than as strictly exact.

[15] *Memoria de Hacienda 1870* 97-98.

[16] *Memoria de Hacienda 1870* 97-98, 101-102.

[17] *Memoria de Hacienda 1832* 79-80; *Memoria de Hacienda 1833* 51-52.

[18] *Memoria de Hacienda 1870* 140-41.

[19] *Memoria de Hacienda 1870* 155, 162-63, 166-67.

[20] M. Dublán and J. M. Lozano, *Legislación mexicana o colección completa de las disposiciones legislativas expedidas desde la independencia de la República mexicana*, 34 vols. (México: Imprenta del Comercio, 1876-1912) 3: 25-28.

[21] David W. Walker, "Kinship, Business and Politics. The Martínez del Río Family in Mexico, 1824-1864," diss., U of Chicago, 1981, 185.

[22] Rosa María Meyer Cosío, "Empresarios, crédito y especulación (1820-1850)," *Banca y poder en México (1800-1925)*, eds. Leonor Ludlow and Carlos Marichal (México: Grijalbo, 1985) 99-117.

[23] The subject of creditor funds is explained in great detail in Walker 288-361.

[24] Walker 309-12.

[25] *Memoria de Hacienda 1841* 19.

[26] For more on this see Tenenbaum, *The Politics of Penury: Debts and Taxes in Mexico, 1821-1856* (Albuquerque: U of New Mexico P, 1986).

[27] Dublán and Lozano 4: 94-97, 134-44, 147-50.

[28] For more on this see Manuel Payno, *México y sus cuestiones financieras con la Inglaterra, la España y la Francia* (México: Imprenta de Ignacio Cumplido, 1862).

[29] Dublán and Lozano 4: no. 2791, 24 December 1844; and 5: 23-25.

[30] Thomas Ewing Cotner, *The Military and Political Career of José Joaquín de Herrera, 1792-1854* (Austin: Institute of Latin American Studies, U of Texas, 1949) 136-37.

[31] The active bonds were converted at 90% of face value; the deferred and debentures at 60%. The government issued an extra $10,676,590 in bonds which it sold to Escandón and MacKintosh for $200,000 cash and some credits. Thomas R. Lill, *The National Debt of Mexico. History and Present Status* (New York: Searle, Nichols & Hill, 1919) 92; Edgar Turlington, *Mexico and her Foreign Creditors* (New York: Columbia UP, 1930) 93; Walker 317-18; *Memoria de Hacienda 1870* 278.

[32] Dublán and Lozano 5: 210-16.

[33] See Michael Costeloe, "The Mexican Church and the Rebellion of the Polkos," *Hispanic American Historical Review* 46 (1966): 170-78. Also José Fernando Ramírez, *Mexico during the War with the United States*, ed. Walter V. Scholes, trans. Elliott B. Scherr (Columbia, Missouri: U of Missouri P, 1950) 104-107. Ramírez claims that the Vicar Capitular Juan Manuel Irisarri paid for the revolt and that the rebels had $93,000 left over after expenses. He blames the Church for the loss of Veracruz to the United States (113) and claims that respect for religion declined after the revolt (114). For more on Irisarri, see Walker 163-64.

[34] Walker 318-19; Meyer Cosío 8-9.

[35] Shanti Oyarzábal Salcedo, "Gregorio Mier y Terán en el país de los especuladores, 1830-1869," *Formación y desarrollo de la burguesía en México. Siglo XIX*, ed. Ciro Cardoso (México: Siglo XXI, 1978) 147-48.

[36] Ramírez 148.

[37] The states in descending order of revenue were México, Veracruz, Sinaloa, Tamaulipas, Jalisco, Zacatecas, San Luis Potosí, Guanajuato, and Puebla. *Memoria de Hacienda 1844*, chart following number 70.

[38] *Memoria de Hacienda 1844*. The percentage is really much higher since much of the total income came from loans.

[39] Dennis Berge, "A Mexican Dilemma: The Mexico City Ayuntamiento and the Question of Loyalty, 1846-1848," *The Hispanic American Historical Review* 50 (1970): 227-56.

[40] Walker 319-20.

[41] For additional information on MacKintosh, see Tenenbaum, "Merchants, Money, and Mischief. The British in Mexico, 1821-1862," *The Americas* 35 (1979): 317-40; Reinhard Liehr, "La deuda exterior de México y los 'merchant bankers' británicos, 1821-1860," *Ibero-Amerikanisches Archiv* 9 (1983): 425-28; D. C. M. Platt, "Finanzas británicas en México (1821-1867)," *Historia mexicana* 32 (1982): 226-61.

[42] These names appear in the Trist Papers in the Library of Congress, Washington, D.C. They are mentioned as visiting Trist or dining with him. They were not mere casual acquaintances.

[43] Nicholas Trist, letter to Secretary of State James Buchanan, 25 October 1847, Trist Papers, Library of Congress, Washington, D.C.

[44] Luis Hargous, letter to Edward Thornton, 3 July 1847, Trist Papers, Library of Congress, Washington, D.C.

⁴⁵ Nicholas P. Trist, letter to Commander in Chief of U.S. Forces, General Winfield Scott, 16 July 1847, Trist Papers, Library of Congress, Washington, D.C.
⁴⁶ Commander in Chief of U.S. Forces, General Winfield Scott, letter to Nicholas P. Trist, 17 July 1847, Trist Papers, Library of Congress, Washington, D.C.
⁴⁷ Nicholas P. Trist, letter to Secretary of State James Buchanan, September 1847, Trist Papers, Library of Congress, Washington, D.C.
⁴⁸ Nicholas P. Trist, letter to Secretary of State James Buchanan, 6 October 1847, Trist Papers, Library of Congress, Washington, D.C.
⁴⁹ Nicholas P. Trist, letter to Secretary of State James Buchanan, December 1847, Trist Papers, Library of Congress, Washington, D.C.
⁵⁰ Nicholas P. Trist, letter to Virginia Trist, 28 November and 4 December 1847, Trist Papers, Library of Congress, Washington, D.C.
⁵¹ Edward Thornton, letter to Nicholas P. Trist, 11 December 1847, Trist Papers, Library of Congress, Washington, D.C.
⁵² George Rives, *The United States and Mexico, 1821–1848*, 2 vols. (New York: Charles Scribner's Sons, 1912) 2: 510; Justin Smith, *The War with Mexico*, 2 vols. (Gloucester, Massachusetts: P. Smith, 1963) 2: 240; Ramón Alcáraz, *The Other Side or Notes for the History of the War*, trans. Albert Ramsey (New York: Burt Franklin, 1970) 312.
⁵³ Nicholas P. Trist, letter to the Mexican Commissioners, 29 January 1848, Trist Papers, Library of Congress, Washington, D.C.
⁵⁴ Justin Smith 2: 240.
⁵⁵ Rives 633.
⁵⁶ Ralph Hidy, *The House of Baring* (Cambridge: Harvard UP, 1949) 583n20; *El Siglo XIX* 1, 2, 4, 6, 8, 9, and 10 October 1848: 1–2.
⁵⁷ James K. Polk, *Diary*, 3 vols., ed. Milo M. Quaife (Chicago: A. C. McClung and Co., 1910) 3: 357–58.
⁵⁸ Rives 2: 633; *National Intelligencer*, 29 February 1848, as cited by John H. Schroeder, *Mr. Polk's War. American Opposition and Dissent, 1846–1848* (Madison: U of Wisconsin P, 1973) 157.

6 Patriarchy and the Status of Women in the Late Nineteenth-Century Southwest

¹ The following essay is published with permission of the University of Notre Dame Press and is adapted from my book *La familia: Chicano Urban Families in the Southwest, 1848 to the Present* (Notre Dame: U of Notre Dame P, 1984).
² Sylvia Marina Arrom, *The Women of Mexico City, 1790–1857* (Stanford: Stanford UP, 1985).
³ Ramón Gutiérrez, "Marriage, Sex, and the Family: Social Change in Colonial New Mexico, 1660–1846," diss., U of Wisconsin, Madison, 1980, 33.
⁴ Verena Martínez-Alier, *Marriage, Class, and Colour in Nineteenth-Century Cuba: A Study of Racial Attitudes and Sexual Values in a Slave Society* (Cambridge: Cambridge UP, 1974) 124.

[5] Frances León Swadesh, *Los primeros pobladores: Hispanic Americans of the Ute Frontier* (Notre Dame: U of Notre Dame P, 1974) 178-79.
[6] Gutiérrez 446-47.
[7] Colin MacLachlan and Jaime Rodríguez, *The Forging of the Cosmic Race: A Reinterpretation of Colonial Mexico* (Berkeley: U of California P, 1980) 238-39.
[8] The Abeyta Family Collection, ms., The Museum of New Mexico, Santa Fe.
[9] Carmen Lucero, "Reminiscences of Carmen Lucero," ts., Arizona Historical Society, Tucson.
[10] Francisca Solano León, "Reminiscences of Francisca Solano León," ts., Arizona Historical Society, Tucson.
[11] José Arnaz, *Recuerdos*, ms., The Bancroft Library, Berkeley.
[12] Antonio Coronel, *La mujer*, ms., The Coronel Collection, Los Angeles County Museum of Natural History, Los Angeles, 229.
[13] *La familia regulada*, fragmentary ms., The Coronel Collection, Los Angeles County Museum of Natural History, Los Angeles.
[14] *La familia regulada* 90, 107.
[15] Arrom 162.
[16] Arrom 172; Arrom (191) believes that the cult of *marianismo*, the idealization of the long-suffering, self-abnegating and morally superior mother, did not emerge in Mexico until the late 1850s, and then mainly due to influences emanating from Victorian Europe.
[17] Gutiérrez 46.
[18] Coronel.
[19] Kathleen M. Gonzales, "The Mexican Family in San Antonio, Texas," thesis, U of Texas, Austin, 1928, 9.
[20] Gonzales 15.
[21] Rodríguez and MacLachlan 248.
[22] Rodríguez and MacLachlan 236.
[23] Lesley Byrd Simpson, *Many Mexicos* (Berkeley: U of California P, 1969) 167-68.
[24] For a review of the Mexican literature on *las heroinas*, see Arrom 4-11.
[25] Alfredo Mirandé and Evangelina Enríquez, *La Chicana: The Mexican American Woman* (Chicago: U of Chicago P, 1979) 64-67; Jane Dysart, "Mexican Women in San Antonio, 1830-1860: The Assimilation Process," *Western Historical Quarterly* 7 (1976): 366. Chicana history after 1900 has continued, in the Mexican tradition, to chronicle the lives of important women in the Southwest and elsewhere. See, for example, the film *La Chicana* by Silvia Morales (1978) which dramatizes the historical importance of such figures as Lucy Gonzales Parsons, Teresa Urrea, La Santa de Cabora, Emma Tenayuca, Dolores Huerta, and others. See also Mirandé and Enríquez (63-75, 221-41) for an overview of Chicanas who escaped the cage of custom.
[26] Arrom found as much in her study of women in Mexico City. She concluded that: "Home life varied considerably for women of different socioeconomic classes, but irrespective of status, it did not revolve exclusively around the nuclear family" (295). The main thesis of her work is that women's lives in Mexico before 1857 can best be understood by enlarging the study beyond the family to the larger society.

[27] For a view of the crises engendered by the Wars of Independence and the years of the Mexican Republic, see Jaime E. Rodríguez O., "Down from Colonialism: Mexico's Nineteenth-Century Crises," *Distinguished Faculty Lecture* (Irvine: U of California P, 1980).

[28] Gutiérrez 368–405, 435, 445–47; Rebecca McDowell Craver, *The Impact of Intimacy: Mexican-Anglo Intermarriage in New Mexico, 1821–1846* (El Paso: Texas Western P, 1982) 6.

[29] Manuel Torres, *Percipecias de la vida californiana*, ms., The Bancroft Collection, U of California, Berkeley. Torres also complained that the number of servants had declined, making life difficult for the californio aristocracy.

[30] Barbara Laslett, "Household Structure on an American Frontier: Los Angeles, California in 1850," *American Journal of Sociology* 81 (1975): 125.

[31] Barbara Laslett, "Social Change and the Family: Los Angeles, California, 1850–1870," *American Sociological Review* 42 (1977): 269–90.

[32] Carl Degler, *At Odds: Women and the Family in America from the Revolution to the Present* (New York: Oxford UP, 1980) 129.

[33] Herbert Gutman, *The Black Family in Slavery and Freedom, 1750–1925* (New York: Pantheon Books, 1976); Elizabeth Pleck, "The Two-Parent Household: Black Family Structure in Late Nineteenth-Century Boston," *The American Family in Social-Historical Perspective*, ed. Michael Gordon (New York: St. Martin's P, 1973) 152–78.

[34] Pleck 444–45, 489.

[35] Laurence A. Glasco, "The Life Cycle and Household Structure of American Ethnic Groups: Irish, German, and Native Born Whites in Buffalo, New York, 1855," *Family and Kin in Urban Communities, 1700–1930*, ed. Tamara K. Hareven (New York: New Viewpoints, 1977) 138.

[36] Degler 129–31.

[37] The Pearson Correlation of the percentage of female-headed households with the percentage of the male work force unemployed was 0.172 with p = .0278.

[38] Joseph F. Park, "The History of Mexican Labor in Arizona during the Territorial Period," diss., U of Arizona, 1961, 149.

[39] Richard Griswold del Castillo, "Health and the Mexican Americans in Los Angeles, 1850–1887," *Journal of Mexican-American History* 4 (1974): 67.

[40] María Josefa Bandini de Carrillo, letter to Cave Couts, 20 November 1864, The Huntington Library, San Marino, California.

[41] Mariano Vallejo, letter to Platon Vallejo, 17 March 1869, The Bancroft Library, Berkeley, California.

[42] James Tafolla, Sr., "Nearing the End of the Trail: The Autobiography of Rev. James Tafolla, Sr.—A Texas Pioneer, 1837–1911," trans. Fidel C. Tafolla, The Tafolla Family Papers, The Benson Library, Mexican-American Collection, U of Texas, Ausin, 71.

[43] Alberto Camarillo, *Chicanos in a Changing Society: From Mexican Pueblos to American Barrios in Santa Barbara and Southern California, 1848–1930* (Cambridge: Harvard UP, 1979) 135.

[44] Virginia Y. McLaughlin, *Family and Community: Italian Immigrants in Buffalo, 1880–1930* (Ithaca: Cornell UP, 1980) 88.

[45] John Briggs found a similar low rate of Italian female-headed households in New York and Kansas City in 1905. He concluded that cultural cohesive-

ness was important in preventing the disorganization of family life among working-class Italian immigrants. See John W. Briggs, *An Italian Passage: Immigrants to Three American Cities, 1890-1930* (New Haven: Yale UP, 1978) 107.

[46] Camarillo 221.

[47] Arnoldo de León, *The Tejano Community, 1836-1900* (Albuquerque: U of New Mexico P, 1982) 95.

[48] Degler 139-40.

[49] Mario García, *Desert Immigrants: The Mexicans of El Paso, 1880-1920* (New Haven: Yale UP, 1981) 200.

[50] Barbara Weslter, "The Cult of True Womanhood: 1820-1860," *The American Family in Social-Historical Perspective*, ed. Michael Gordon (New York: St. Martin's P, 1978) 313.

[51] For a detailed study of the ways in which the Victorian expectations regarding women led to the creation of the modern companionate family, see Robert L. Griswold, *Family and Divorce in California, 1850-1890: Victorian Illusions and Everyday Realities* (Albany: State U of New York P, 1982). Griswold argues that the Victorians' cult of true womanhood gave women an elevated status in society and a new self-confidence that led to more egalitarian expectations in marriage. His study was based on a sample of divorce records for San Mateo and Santa Clara County during the period 1850-90 and did not include any significant number of Mexican Americans. His findings are probably most applicable to the upper- and middle-class assimilated or assimilating Mexican Americans.

Bibliography

Aguirre Beltrán, Gonzalo. *La población negra de México.* 2nd ed. México: Fondo de Cultura Económica, 1972.

Alamán, Lucas. *Historia de Méjico.* 5 vols. México: Editorial Jus, 1968.

Alcáraz, Ramón. *The Other Side or Notes for the History of the War.* Trans. Albert Ramsey. New York: Burt Franklin, 1970.

Anna, Timothy E. *The Fall of the Royal Government in Mexico City.* Lincoln: U of Nebraska P, 1978.

———. "Francisco Novella and the Last Stand of the Royal Army in New Spain." *Hispanic American Historical Review* 51 (1971): 92-111.

Archer, Christon I. "The Royalist Army in New Spain: Civil-Military Relationships." *Journal of Latin American Studies* 13.1 (1981): 79-80.

Arrom, Silvia Marina. *The Women of Mexico City, 1790-1857.* Stanford: Stanford UP, 1985.

Aubrey, Henry G. "The National Income of Mexico." *I.A.S.I. Estadística* (June 1950): 185-98.

Bataillon, Claude. *Las regiones geográficas en México.* México: Siglo XXI, 1969.

Bazant, Jan. *Cinco haciendas mexicanas.* México: El Colegio de México, 1975.

Berge, Dennis. "A Mexican Dilemma: The Mexico City Ayuntamiento and the Question of Loyalty, 1846-1848." *Hispanic American Historical Review* 50 (1970): 227-56.

Bourdeau, Georges. *Le Liberalisme.* París: Editions du Seuil, 1979.

Brading, David. *Haciendas and Ranchos in the Mexican Bajío: León, 1700-1860.* Cambridge: Cambridge UP, 1978.

———. "La minería de la plata en el siglo XVIII: El caso de Bolaños." *Historia mexicana* 18 (1969): 317-33.

———. *Miners and Merchants in Bourbon Mexico, 1780-1810.* Cambridge: Cambridge UP, 1971.

———. "Mexican Silver in the 18th Century: The Revival of Zacatecas." *Hispanic American Historical Review* 53 (1973): 387-414.

Briggs, John W. *An Italian Passage: Immigrants to Three American Cities, 1890-1930.* New Haven: Yale UP, 1978.

Burke, Edmund. *Reflections on the Revolution in France and the Proceedings in Certain Societies in London Relative to that Event.* Ed. Conor Cruise O'Brien. Great Britain: Pelican Classics, 1969.

Bustamante, Carlos María. *Cuadro histórico de la Revolución de Independencia,* 3 vols. México: Cámara de Diputados, 1961.

Calderón de la Barca, Fanny. *Life in Mexico.* New York: Doubleday, 1966.

Camarillo, Alberto. *Chicanos in a Changing Society: From Mexican Pueblos to American Barrios in Santa Barbara and Southern California, 1848-1930.* Cambridge: Harvard UP, 1979.

Christiansen, E. *The Origins of Military Power in Spain, 1800-1854.* Oxford: Oxford UP, 1967.

Coatsworth, John H. "Obstacles to Economic Growth in Nineteenth-Century Mexico." *American Historical Review* 83 (1978): 80-100.

Congar, Ives M. *Sacerdocio y laicado.* Madrid: Editoral Estela, 1964.

Costeloe, Michael. "The Mexican Church and the Rebellion of the Polkos." *Hispanic American Historical Review* 46 (1966): 170-78.

———. *La Primera República Federal de México, 1824-1835.* México: Fondo de Cultura Económica, 1975.

Cotner, Thomas Ewing. *The Military and Political Career of José Joaquín de Herrera, 1792-1854.* Austin: U of Texas, Institute of Latin American Studies, 1949.

Craver, Rebecca McDowell. *The Impact of Intimacy: Mexican-Anglo Intermarriage in New Mexico, 1821-1846.* El Paso: Texas Western, 1982.

Cross, Harry. "Living Standards in Rural Nineteenth-Century Mexico." *Journal of Latin American Studies* 10 (1978): 1-19.

Degler, Carl. *At Odds: Women and the Family in America from the Revolution to the Present.* New York: Oxford UP, 1980.

De León, Arnoldo. *The Tejano Community, 1836-1900.* Albuquerque: U of New Mexico P, 1982.

Denzinger, Enrique. *El Magisterio de la Iglesia.* Barcelona: Herder, 1963.

Díaz Díaz, Fernando. *Caudillos y caciques.* México: El Colegio de México, 1972.

Dublán, M., and J. M. Lozano. *Legislación mexicana o colección completa de las disposiciones legislativas expedidas desde la independencia de la República mexicana.* 34 vols. México: Imprenta del Comercio, 1876-1912.

Dysart, Jane. "Mexican Women in San Antonio, 1830-1860: The Assimilation Process." *Western Historical Quarterly* 7 (1976): 366.

Flores Caballero, Romeo. *La contrarrevolución en la independencia.* México: El Colegio de México, 1969.

———. *Counterrevolution, The Role of the Spaniards in the Independence of Mexico, 1804-1838.* Trans. Jaime E. Rodríguez O. Lincoln: U of Nebraska P, 1974.

García, Mario. *Desert Immigrants: The Mexicans of El Paso, 1880-1920.* New Haven: Yale UP, 1981.

Glasco, Laurence A. "The Life Cycle and Household Structure of American Ethnic Groups: Irish, German, and Native Born Whites in Buffalo, New

York, 1855." *Family and Kin in Urban Communities, 1700-1930.* Ed. Tamara K. Hareven. New York: New Viewpoints, 1977.

Gonzales, Kathleen M. "The Mexican Family in San Antonio, Texas." Thesis. U of Texas, Austin, 1928.

González, María del Rufugio. *Historia del derecho mexicano.* México: Universidad Nacional Autónoma de México, 1981.

González Navarro, Moisés. *Anatomía del poder en México.* México: El Colegio de México, 1977.

González Reyna, Jenaro. *Riqueza minera y yacimientos minerales en México.* México: Banco de México, 1947.

Griswold, Robert L. *Family and Divorce in California, 1850-1890: Victorian Illusions and Everyday Realities.* Albany: State U of New York P, 1982.

Griswold del Castillo, Richard. "Health and the Mexican Americans in Los Angeles, 1850-1887." *Journal of Mexican-American History* 4 (1974): 67.

———. *La Familia: Chicano Urban Families in the Southwest, 1848 to the Present.* Notre Dame: U of Notre Dame P, 1984.

Gutiérrez, Ramón. "Marriage, Sex, and the Family: Social Change in Colonial New Mexico, 1660-1846." Diss. U of Wisconsin P, 1980.

Gutman, Herbert. *The Black Family in Slavery and Freedom, 1750-1925.* New York: Pantheon Books, 1976.

Hale, Charles. *El liberalismo en México de la época de Mora.* México: Siglo XXI, 1978.

———. *Mexican Liberalism in the Age of Mora, 1821-1853.* New Haven: Yale UP, 1968.

Hamill, Hugh M. "Was the Mexican Independence Movement a Revolution?" *Dos revoluciones: México y los Estados Unidos.* México: Banamex, 1976.

———. *The Hidalgo Revolt: Prelude to Mexican Independence.* Gainesville: U of Florida P, 1966.

———. "Royalist Counter-insurgency in the Mexican War of Independence: The Lessons of 1811." *Hispanic American Historical Review* 53 (1973): 486.

Hamnett, Brian R. "Anastasio Bustamante y la Guerra de Independencia, 1810-1821." *Historia mexicana* 28 (1979): 515-45.

———. *Revolución y contrarrevolución en México y el Perú. Liberalismo realeza y separatismo 1800-1824.* México: Fondo de Cultura Económica, 1978.

Handling, Oscar. *La verdad en la Historia.* México: Fondo de Cultura Económica, 1982.

Harris, Charles H. *A Mexican Family Empire: The Latifundio of the Sánchez-Navarro Navarro Family, 1765-1867.* Austin: U of Texas P, 1975.

Herrera Canales, Inés. *El comercio exterior de México, 1821-1875.* México: El Colegio de México, 1977.

Hidy, Ralph. *The House of Baring.* Cambridge: Harvard UP, 1949.

Hintze, Otto. *Historia de las formas políticas.* Madrid: Ediciones de la Revista de Occidente, 1976.

Humboldt, Alexander von. *Essai politique sur le royaume de la Nouvelle-Espagne.* 5 vols. Paris: F. Schoell, 1811.

Keremitsis, Dawn. *La industria textil mexicana en el siglo XIX.* México: Secretaría de Educación Pública, 1973.

Ladd, Doris M. *The Mexican Nobility at Independence.* Austin: U of Texas, Institute of Latin American Studies, 1976.

Laslett, Barbara. "Household Structure on an American Frontier: Los Angeles, California in 1850." *American Journal of Sociology* 81 (1975): 125.

———. "Social Change and the Family: Los Angeles, California, 1850–1870." *American Sociological Review* 42 (1977): 269-90.

Lavrin, Asunción. "The Execution of the Law of Consolidation in New Spain." *Hispanic American Historical Review* 52 (1973): 27-49.

Lerdo de Tejada, Miguel. *Comercio exterior de México desde la Conquista hasta hoy.* 2nd ed., México: Banco Nacional de Comercio Exterior, 1976.

Lerner, Victoria. "La problación de la Nueva España." *Historia mexicana* 28 (1968): 327-46.

Liehr, Reinhard. "La deuda exterior de México y los 'Merchant bankers' británicos, 1821-1860." *Ibero-Amerikanisches Archiv* 9 (1983): 425-28.

Lill, Thomas R. *The National Debt of Mexico. History and Present Status.* New York: Searle, Nichols & Hill, 1919.

López Cámara, Francisco. *La estructura económica y social de México en la época de la Reforma.* México: Siglo XXI, 1967.

Lynn, G. F. *Journal of a Residence and Tour in the Republic of Mexico.* 2 vols. London: J. Murray, 1828.

MacLachlan, Colin, and Jaime E. Rodríguez O. *The Forging of the Cosmic Race: A Reinterpretation of Colonial Mexico.* Berkeley: U of California P, 1980.

Macune, Charles. *El Estado de México y la Federación mexicana 1823-1835.* México: Fondo de Cultura Económica, 1978.

McDowell Craver, Rebecca. *The Impact of Intimacy: Mexican-Anglo Intermarriage in New Mexico, 1821-1846.* El Paso: Texas Western P, 1982.

McLaughlin, Virginia Y. *Family and Community: Italian Immigrants in Buffalo, 1880-1930.* Ithaca: Cornell UP, 1980.

Martínez-Alier, Verena. *Marriage, Class, and Colour in Nineteenth-Century Cuba: A Study of Racial Attitudes and Sexual Values in a Slave Society.* Cambridge: Cambridge UP, 1974.

Marx, Karl, and Friedrich Engels. *Collected Works.* 16 vols. New York: International Publishers, 1976.

Mirandé, Alfredo, and Evangelina Enríquez. *La Chicana: The Mexican American Woman.* Chicago: U of Chicago P, 1979.

Mora, José María Luis. *Obras sueltas.* Vol. I. París: Libería de la Rosa, 1837.

Moreno de los Arcos, Roberto. "La última Nueva España." *La formación del Estado mexicano.* Ed. María del Refugio González. México: Editorial Porrúa, 1984. 15-29.

———. "Las instituciones de la industria minera novohispana." In Miguel León-Portilla, et al. *La Minería en México*. México: Universidad Nacional Autónoma de México, (1978): 68–164.

Munguía, Clemente de Jesús. *Del Derecho Natural en sus principios comunes y en sus diversas ramificaciones o sea, Curso elemental de Derecho Natural y de gentes, público, político, constitucional y principios de legislación*. 3 vols. México: Imprenta de la Voz de la Religión, 1849.

Noriega, Alfonso. *El pensamiento conservador y el conservadurismo mexicano*. 2 vols. México: Universidad Nacional Autónoma de México, 1972.

O'Gorman, Edmundo. *México: el trauma de su historia*. México: Universidad Nacional Autónoma de México, 1977.

Ortiz Valadés, Salvador. *La arriería en México*. México: n.p., 1929.

Palmade, Guy, "La época de la burguesía," *Historia Universal*. Madrid: Siglo XXI, 1976.

Park, Joseph F. "The History of Mexican Labor in Arizona during the Territorial Period." Diss., U of Arizona P, 1961.

Pastor, Rodolfo. "De la Autonomía Ilustrada a la Revolución." *México y su historia*. México: Editorial Uthea, 1984. vol. 4.

Payno, Manuel. *México y sus cuestiones financieras con la Inglaterra, la España y la Francia*. México: Imprenta de Ignacio Cumplido, 1862.

Pereyra, Carlos. *Historia de la América Española*. Madrid: Editorial Saturnino Calleja, 1924.

Platt, D. C. M. "Finanzas Británicas en México (1821–1867)." *Historia mexicana* 32 (1982): 226–61.

Pleck, Elizabeth. "The Two-Parent Household: Black Family Structure in Late Nineteenth-Century Boston," *The American Family in Social-Historical Perspective*. Ed. Michael Gordon. New York: St. Martin's P, 1973: 152–78.

Poinsett, Joel R. *Notes on Mexico*. Philadelphia: H. C. Carey and I. Lea, 1824.

Polk, James K. *Diary*. 3 vols. Ed. Milo M. Quaife. Chicago: A. C. McClung and Co., 1910.

Potash, Robert. *El Banco de Avío de México: El fomento de la industria, 1821–1846*. México: Fondo de Cultura Económica, 1959.

Quirate, Martín. *El problema religioso en México*. México: Instituto Nacional de Antropología e Historia, 1967.

Quirós, José María. *Memoria de estatuto*. Veracruz, 1817.

Ramírez, Felipe Tena. *Leyes fundamentales de México (1808–1975)*. 6a. ed. México: Porrúa, 1975.

Ramírez, José Fernando. *Mexico during the War with the United States*. Ed. Walter V. Scholes. Trans. Elliott B. Scherr. Columbia, Missouri: U of Missouri P, 1950.

Randall, Robert W. *Real del Monte: A British Mining Venture in Mexico*. Austin: U of Texas P, 1972.

Rees, Peter. *Transportes y comercio entre México y Veracruz*. México: Secretaría de Educación Pública, 1976.

Reyes Heroles, Jesús. *El liberalismo mexicano.* 3 vols. México: Fondo de Cultura Económica, 1974.
Reynolds, Clark W. *The Mexican Economy: Twentieth-Century Structure and Growth.* New Haven: Yale UP, 1970.
Ricard, Robert. *La conquista espiritual de México.* México: Editorial Jus, 1974.
Ringrose, David. *Transportation and Economic Stagnation in Spain, 1750-1850.* Durham: Duke UP, 1970.
Rives, Infant George. *The United States and Mexico, 1821-1848.* 2 vols. New York: Charles Scribner's Sons, 1912.
Robertson, William S. *Iturbide of Mexico.* Durham: Duke UP, 1952.
Rodríguez O., Jaime E. *The Emergence of Spanish America: Vicente Rocafuerte and Spanish Americanism, 1808-1832.* Berkeley: U of California P, 1975.
Rosenzweig Hernández, Fernando. "La economía novohispana a comenzar el siglo XIX." *Ciencias políticas y sociales* 9 (1963): 455-94.
Salcedo, Shanti Oyarzábal. "Gregorio Mier y Terán en el país de los especuladores, 1830-1869." *Formación y desarrollo de la burguesía en México, Siglo XIX.* Ed. Ciro Cardoso. México: Siglo XXI, 1978.
Schroeder, John H. *Mr. Polk's War. American Opposition and Dissent, 1846-1848.* Madison: U of Wisconsin P, 1973.
Simpson, Lesley Byrd. *Many Mexicos.* Berkeley: U of California P, 1969.
Sims, Harold D. *Descolonización en México. El conflicto entre mexicanos y españoles, 1821-1831.* México: Fondo de Cultura Económica, 1982.
———. *La expulsión de los españoles de México, 1812-1828.* México: Fondo de Cultura Económica, 1974.
Smith, Justin Harvey. *The War with Mexico.* 2 vols. Gloucester, Mass: P. Smith, 1963.
Soetbeer, Adolf. *Edelmetall-produktion und werthverhältniss zwischen gold und silver.* Götha, 1874.
Swadesh, Frances León. *Los primeros pobladores: Hispanic Americans of the Ute Frontier.* Notre Dame: U of Notre Dame P, 1974.
Tafolla, James, Sr. "Nearing the End of the Trial: The Autobiography of Rev. James Tafolla, Sr. — A Texas Pioneer, 1837-1911." Trans. Fidel C. Tafolla. The Tafolla Family Papers. The Benson Library, Mexican-American Collection. U of Texas, Austin.
Tamayo, Jorge L. *Benito Juárez. Documentos, discursos y correspondencia.* México: Editorial Libros de México, 1972. Vol. 4.
———. *Geografía general de México.* 4 vols. 2nd ed. México: Instituto Mexicano de Investigaciones Económicas, 1962.
Tenenbaum, Barbara A. "Merchants, Money and Mischief. The British in Mexico, 1821-1862." *The Americas* 35 (1979): 317-40.
———. *The Politics of Penury: Debts and Taxes in Mexico, 1821-1856.* Albuquerque: U of New Mexico P, 1986.
TePaske, John J., Jose Hernández, and Mari Luz Hernández Palomo. *La Real Hacienda de Nueva España: La real caja de México (1576-1816).* México: Departamento de Investigacions Históricas, 1976.

Torres, Manuel. *Peripecias de la vida Californiana.* Ms. The Bancroft Collection. U of California, Berkeley.
Touchard, Jean. *Historia de las ideas políticas.* Madrid: Editorial Tecnos, 1969.
Turlington, Edgar. *Mexico and her Foreign Creditors.* New York: Columbia UP, 1930.
Valadés, José C. *El pensamiento político de Benito Juárez.* México: Librería de Manual Porrúa, 1972.
Villegas, Abelardo. *México en el horizonte liberal.* México: Universidad Nacional Autónoma de México, 1981.
Walker, David W. "Kinship, Business and Politics. The Martínez del Río Family in Mexico, 1824–1864." Diss., U of Chicago, 1981.
Ward, Henry G. *Mexico in 1827.* 2 vols. 2nd ed. London: Henry Colburn, 1829.
Weber, Max. *Economía y sociedad.* 3 vols. México: Fondo de Cultura Económica, 1944.
Welter, Barbara. "The Cult of True Womanhood: 1820–1860," *The American Family in Social-Historical Perspective.* Ed. Michael Gordon. New York: St. Martin's P, 1978.

Index

Adame, Jorge, 62
Aguirre, Matías de, 33
Alamán, Lucas, 64, 73
Alcaraz, Ramón, 82
Alvarez, Melchor, 30
Anaya, Pedro María, 77
Anza, Juan Bautista de, 90
Arballo y Gutiérrez, María Feliciana, 90
Archer, Christon I., 4
Arista, Mariano, 83
Armijo, Gabriel, 34, 40
Arnaz, José, 88
Arrom, Silvia Marina, 85, 88
Asencio, Pedro (El Indio), 34, 39
Asisi, Francisco de, 39, 40
Ateaga, Juan de, 40
Atristain, Miguel, 82

Bacon, Francis, 65
Bandini de Carrillo, María Josefa, 95
Bankhead, Charles, 77, 79
Barragán, Miguel, 42
Becerra, Doña Josefa, 90
Birones de Miranda, Juana, 91
Boixo, Juan, 35
Bravo, Nicolás, 77
Buchanan, James, 79, 80
Burke, Edmund, 56, 63, 65
Bustamante, Anastasio, 41, 73, 75

Calleja, Félix, 25, 27-29, 31, 69
Camarillo, Alberto, 95
Canseco, Manuel María, 75
Carlos III, 48
Castillo y Bustamante, Joaquín, 31
Charles III, 69
Comonfort, Ignacio, 83
Coronel, Antonio, 88
Cortázar, Luis, 41

Cruz, Sor Juana Inés de la, 90

Davison, Lionel, 80
Degler, Carl, 98
Doyle, Percy, 82
Drusina, Guillermo de, 80

Echeagaray, José María, 31
Echeverría, Francisco Javier, 75
Elzora, Agustín de, 42
Erazu, Doña Catalina de, 90
Escandón, Manuel, 77

Fages, Doña Eulalia, 90
Fernando VII, 30, 31, 37

Galeana de Valadés, Patricia, 4, 5
Garay, Antonio, 74
García, Mario, 98
Glasco, Laurence, 93
Gómez Farías, Valentín, 73, 77
González, Kathleen, 89
González, María del Refugio, 5, 45
Griswold del Castillo, Richard, 5
Guerrero, Vicente, 34, 72
Gutiérrez, Ramón, 86-88
Gutman, Herbert, 93

Habsburgo, Fernando Maximiliano de, 52
Hargous, Luis, 80
Haro y Tamariz, Antonio, 77
Hermanos, Rosas, 78
Herrera, José Joaquín de, 41, 70, 77, 83
Hevia, Francisco de, 42
Hidalgo, Miguel, 24-26, 48
Houston, Samuel, 82

Ignacio, Coronel, 89
Iturbe, Francisco María, 74, 78

INDEX

Iturbide, Agustín, 31, 34, 36, 40, 41 43, 70
Izquierdo, Manuel, 36
José II, 52
Juárez, Benito, 50, 52-54, 79, 83
Juzgado General de Naturales, 60
Kesner, Thomas, 98
Laslett, Barbara, 92
Lefevre, George, 56, 58
Lerdo de Tejada, Sebastián, 53
Linares, Antonio, 37, 42
Liñan, Pascual, 35, 42
Llano, Ciriaco de, 33, 38, 41, 43
López de Santa Anna, Antonio, 39, 40, 73, 75-76, 78, 81
Luaces, Domingo, 35-36, 42-43
Lucero, Carmen, 87
Lyon, G. F., 16

MacKintosh, Ewen Clark, 78, 80-83
MacLachlan, Colin, 90
La Malinche (Doña Marina), 90
Marqués de Campo Sagrado, 30
Márquez y Donallo, José Joaquín, 42
Martínez-Alier, Verena, 86
Marx, Karl, 12
McLaughlin, Virginia Yans, 96
Merino, Manuel, 41
Mier y Terán, Gregorio, 78
Mora, José María Luis, 15, 49
Morelos, José María, 24-25, 29, 48
Moreno, Roberto, 58
Moreno y Daoiz, José, 30
Moreno y Daoiz, Tomás, 30
Munguía, Clemente de Jesús, 64-66

Napoleón III, 52
Novella, Francisco de, 43

Obregón, Antonio de, 9
Ocampo, Melchor, 50, 83
Ortega, Francisco, 51
Ortiz de Domínguez, Doña Josefa, 90

Pacheco, José Ramón, 81

Pakenham, Richard, 76
Palmerston, (Lord), 80
Paredes y Arrillaga, Mariano, 77
Parres, Joaquín, 42
Payno, Manuel, 83
Peña y Peña, Manuel de la, 77, 81
Peño, Bartolomé, 42
Pío IX, 66
Pleck, Elizabeth, 93
Poinsett, Joel, 16
Polk, James Knox, 77-78, 81, 83
Prieto, Guillermo, 54, 83

Quirarte, Martín, 50
Quirós, José María, 15

Rafols, Juan, 34, 39, 42
Rodríguez, Alférez Santiago, 34
Rodríguez O., Jaime E., 90
Rodríguez de San Miguel, Juan N., 64
Rondero, Juan, 78, 83
Rosa, Luis de la, 76
Rousseau, Jean Jacques, 57
Ruíz de Apodaca, Juan, 31, 33, 35-36, 43

Salas, Mariano, 77
Scott, Winfield, 78-82
Solano León, Francisca, 87

Tafolla, James, 95
Taylor, Zachary, 78, 83
Tenenbaum, Barbara A., 5
Thorton, Edward, 79-83
Triqueros, Ignacio, 75
Trist, Nicholas, 79-83
Trist, Virginia, 82

Venadito, Conde de (See also Venegas, Francisco Javier), 38-43
Venegas, Francisco Javier, 30
Victoria, Guadalupe, 11, 70, 83
Voltaire (François-Marie Arouet), 57
Von Humboldt, Alexander, 3, 22

Zavala, Lorenzo de, 3, 72
Zurutuzu, Antonio, 74